RES COGITANS

An Essay in
Rational Psychology

CONTEMPORARY PHILOSOPHY

General Editor
Max Black, Cornell University

RES COGITANS

An Essay in Rational Psychology

By Zeno Vendler

Cornell University Press

ITHACA AND LONDON

All rights reserved. Except for brief quotations in a review, this book, or parts thereof, must not be reproduced in any form without permission in writing from the publisher. For information address Cornell University Press, 124 Roberts Place, Ithaca, New York 14850.

First published 1972 by Cornell University Press.
Published in the United Kingdom by Cornell University Press Ltd.,
2–4 Brook Street, London W1Y 1AA.

International Standard Book Number 0-8014-0743-5
Library of Congress Catalog Card Number 72-3182

PRINTED IN THE UNITED STATES OF AMERICA
BY VAIL-BALLOU PRESS, INC.

Librarians: Library of Congress cataloging information appears on the last page of the book.

For Gilbert Ryle,
who set the example

Preface

A few years ago I was asked to write a review of J. L. Austin's *How to Do Things with Words* for *Foundations of Language* (III [1967], 303–310). In rereading those lectures (which I had also had the privilege of hearing viva voce), I realized that the grammatical criterion Austin uses for gathering illocutionary verbs is too loose: it catches a vast and important group of other verbs as well. As I thought about the matter later on, the implications of this discovery opened up a whole perspective on the relation of speech and thought—a distinctly rationalistic, Cartesian perspective. Since at the same time I was aware of the emergence of a similar trend in contemporary linguistics (originating in the works of Professor Chomsky), I tried to combine my results with ideas derived from this source. The upshot of my investigations has turned out to be more than I had bargained for: a nearly complete and fairly well organized account of man as a thinking and talking being, a new articulation of the concept of mind.

If the account I give is right, then Professor Ryle's *Concept*

Preface

of Mind is wrong, as are all forms of empiricism and behaviorism in philosophical psychology. Moreover, if what I say about language and speech is correct, then what Wittgenstein said about them is not. These facts may justify my prolonged—and sometimes tiring—interest in the problems treated in this book.

Since I could not do much else in these last years, and since it is hard to remain silent for a long time, I have published a few details before completing the whole work. The article "Say What You Think," which gives a glimpse of my original idea, appeared in *Studies in Thought and Language*, edited by J. L. Cowan (Tucson: University of Arizona Press, 1970); the lecture "Word and Concept," which is a shorter version of Chapter VI of this book, is included in the *Royal Institute of Philosophy Lectures, 1969–1970*, edited by G. N. A. Vesey (London: Macmillan-St. Martin's Press, 1971); and a part of Chapter VII appeared in the *Canadian Journal of Philosophy* (published by the Canadian Association for Publishing in Philosophy), I (September 1971), under the title "Descartes on Sensation." I wish to express my gratitude for the gracious permission I received from the editors of these publications to use, and in some cases to reprint, the content of these papers.

In addition I owe many thanks to the Canada Council for generous grants-in-aid, to the Sub-Faculty of Philosophy of Oxford University for its hospitality, and to the many persons, colleagues and students, who helped me with advice and criticism. In this regard I am especially grateful to Professors R. M. Hare and Gilbert Ryle. Finally, to the *genius loci* of the great island of Madeira, my thanks for taking the sting out of the work of thought and writing.

University of Calgary

ZENO VENDLER

viii

Contents

RES COGITANS

An Essay in
Rational Psychology

Parler, est expliquer ses pensées par des signes, que les hommes ont inuentez à ce dessein. . . . C'est pourquoy on ne peut bien comprendre les diuerses sortes de significations, qui sont enfermées dans les mots, qu'on n'ait bien compris auparauant ce qui se passe dans nos pensées, puis que les mots n'ont esté inuentez que pour les faire connoistre.

Grammaire Générale et Raisonnée

(To speak is to express one's thoughts by means of signs that man invented for this purpose. . . . For this reason one cannot really understand the varieties of meaning contained in words without having at the same time a correct understanding of what goes on in our minds, since the sole aim of inventing words has been to make it known to others.)

I

Speech and Thought: An Introduction

1. It is a commonplace among psychologists, linguists, and philosophers that speech and thought are closely related. The universal and abiding interest in the theory of linguistic relativism illustrates this point clearly enough. Yet, if one looks closer, one realizes that the awareness of this link has actually diminished in modern times. Up to the late scholastic period, and then again during the rationalist era, philosophers regarded speech, essentially and by definition, as the expression of thought. Needless to say, this view is quite alien to our contemporaries. Accordingly we are often told that the medievals and the rationalists were insensitive to the importance of language, and that it was only through the rise of empiricism that we came to appreciate the role of language on its own. Yes indeed—but as a result of the triumph of empiricism the relation of speech and thought has become a major problem, burdening the conscience not only of philosophers but also of the new breed of behavioral and social scientists.

Res Cogitans

What has happened, of course, is that the onset of empiricism has radically changed the concept of thought, so that the traditional view about speech as the expression of thought has lost its appeal, if not its very possibility. If thought is nothing but the stream of consciousness we experience, the succession of images we witness on the private stage of the mind, then the problem of how to connect this with the public manifestations of speech will indeed loom large. If speech is to remain the expression of thought, then, obviously, associations must be established between the elements of thought (roughly, ideas) and the elements of speech (roughly, words). As centuries of effort have failed to produce a satisfactory account along these lines, more courageous souls in more recent times have abandoned the traditional view altogether and have come to regard speech as a part of man's overt, social behavior, letting thought take care of itself beyond the pale of respectable science or, more tolerantly, letting the philosophers take care of it.

2. I have no intention of spelling out in detail, at this point, what is wrong with this radical view. I merely indicate its main shortcoming as a theory of language: it fails to explain what it is to say something and what it is to understand something said. For, given its presuppositions, the radical theory is bound to represent saying something as producing an utterance of a certain description in certain circumstances, and it is bound to approach understanding in terms of reacting to such an utterance produced by others. But, as I shall have the opportunity to show later on, the mere production of an utterance does not amount, in any circumstances, to the act of saying something (except in a trivial and irrelevant sense), if the speaker does not understand what he is "saying"; moreover, understanding what one is saying, or what somebody else has

said, cannot be construed at all as acting or reacting in one way or another. Since the mastery of language consists in the ability to say things, and to understand things said, this shortcoming essentially disqualifies the radical view as a theory of language.

Still less needs to be said now of the less radical, "association-ist" position. It has been generally, and deservedly, abandoned because of its incurable weakness in dealing with linguistic structure, abstract terms, and the like. Later on, for good measure, I shall point out some even more fundamental troubles besetting this theory.

3. I have claimed above that what shattered the traditional harmony of speech and thought was the development of a new concept of thought and thinking by the empiricists. It would be an easy task to show that this new notion does not agree with commonsense beliefs, or, if one prefers another idiom, that it is not faithful to the ordinary use of the words *thinking* and *thought*. This fact, however, would not, by itself, discredit the empiricist position in the relevant respect. For many an "artificial" concept did and will do creditable service in helping our understanding in many a field, including philosophy. The point is, however, that the old concept of thought, superseded by the empiricist one in the main stream of philosophical development, albeit not in the common sense of mankind, remains the one that is needed, that is in fact indispensable to the comprehension of what it is to say something, what it is to understand something said, and consequently to the very notion of what speech and language are.

In trying to relocate or rebuild this concept of thought one could follow many paths. One might trace it through the writings of ancient and medieval thinkers and then follow its decay

3

through the rise of empiricism. Or one might start from scratch and rediscover the concept by using the methods of ordinary language philosophy. I shall not take either of these roads, not only because I might be lacking the erudition necessary to take the first and the patience and sensitivity required for the second, but also, and mainly, because my present concern itself offers a shortcut: the full analysis of the notions of saying something and understanding what one said inevitably involves a concept which, as I will show in detail, essentially corresponds to the Cartesian idea of thought and thinking.

I have selected Descartes' views for special consideration, because, in the first place, he is by far the most articulate representative of what I have called the traditional position. No wonder, since the concept of thinking lies at the very center of his philosophy. For the same reason, it is to be expected that a new understanding of this notion is bound to lead us to a reappraisal of his whole doctrine of man, the thinking thing. Having shed the biases of empiricism and behaviorism, which affected Descartes' critics from Hobbes to Ryle, we will be able to achieve a sympathetic understanding of his views, sharing his momentous insights but also realizing his own biases and prejudices. To know a philosopher, it is not enough to know what he said, or even to be able to guess what he would have said on this or that issue; one also must have an idea of what he *should* have said instead of what he actually did, had he been wholly faithful to his own principles. And Descartes is a philosopher worth knowing.

4. There is one more reason recommending the reverse procedure I intend to follow. Going this way we do not have to start from scratch. The idea of saying something, at least, has been admirably treated by J. L. Austin, and the notion of an "illocu-

tionary act" is generally known and widely discussed among philosophers and linguists alike. So we can set out from a familiar landmark.

Austin's work is the first word on this important subject, not the last. It has its shortcomings, which have to be corrected before moving on. Fortunately, some recent developments in linguistics, not yet available to him, make this task possible and even easy; once more, as a result of progress, some defects of ingenuity can be corected by humble routine. Moreover—an unexpected boon—the very correction of one of Austin's oversights will give us the first push toward the goal we have set out to achieve.

II

On Saying Something

1. Falling through Austin's prism the concept of saying something spreads out in a spectrum of illocutionary acts. These acts consist in the issuing of an utterance with a certain illocutionary force.[1] All "happy" or "successful" utterances are endowed with such a force in addition to their meaning (i.e., sense and reference, as he puts it). These forces specify how the utterance in question is intended to be taken—that is, what natural effect (cognitive, motive, social or legal) it is intended to have, and, accordingly, in what dimensions (truth, feasibility, propriety, and so on) it is supposed to be assessed; whether, for instance, it has the "force" of a statement, a warning, a promise, an order, and so forth.

In most cases the illocutionary force remains implicit; more often than not, in a given situation, the speaker need not explicitly specify how the utterance is to be taken: the circumstances and the context may be sufficient to decide. In others

[1] J. L. Austin, *How to Do Things with Words*.

the speaker may give a hint, or more than a hint, by employing certain linguistic media, such as a suitable intonation pattern, sentence transform, or performative verb.[2] Think of the various ways in which a superior officer might order his subordinate to occupy the city: *You will occupy the city* (only the context and, possibly, the intonation pattern distinguishes this from a mere forecast); *Occupy the city!* (here a transform, the imperative, is used in addition to the intonation); *I order you to occupy the city* (in this case he employs a performative verb). Similar examples could be produced for questions, warnings, promises, and the like.

Among these media, the use of performative verbs is the least ambiguous and the most versatile; transforms and intonation patterns are far more restricted in power and variety. It appears, moreover, that whatever the other devices can do, the use of a suitable performative verb can do, but not the other way around. Consequently, from a methodological point of view, it is profitable to regard the utterance prefixed by such a verb as the "normal form" of a performative utterance, that is, of an utterance endowed with an illocutionary force. Implicit performatives, which lack such verbs, have their force "because, in so far as and when they are linked in 'origin' with these special explicit performative verbs like 'promise,' 'pronounce,' 'find,' etc."[3] Since, as I mentioned above, Austin accords illocutionary forces to all "happy" utterances, his implied doctrine is a sweeping generalization: the normal form of all "happy" utterances of the language will contain a performative verb prefixing the substance

---

[2] I shall call all "those verbs which make explicit . . . the illocutionary force of an utterance" (*ibid.*, p. 149) *performative* verbs. My framework is Austin's "general theory," in which the performative-constative distinction of the first half of his book has no special place.

[3] *Ibid.*, p. 61.

of the utterance.[4] If this is so, then the list of performative verbs
will amount to the list of illocutionary forces discernible in a
given language. This connection explains why Austin ends the
second half of his lectures, in which he is primarily concerned
with illocutionary forces, by compiling a catalogue of performative verbs.

2. We may recall that Austin's investigations begin with an
attempt to draw a distinction between "performative" and "con-
stative" utterances. As this task cannot be accomplished to his
satisfaction, he develops the theory of illocutionary acts, that is,
of illocutionary forces accompanying all "happy" or "successful"
utterances. In this new perspective the performative-constative
distinction fades away and what he previously called "performative" utterances retain no special status except for a stronger
emphasis on some illocutionary force or another. Nevertheless,
and exactly because of this strong emphasis, the intuitive notion of an illocutionary act remains dependent upon the previously described characteristics of performative utterances. Austin
suggests a fair number of such marks, but I select three of them,
which are given great weight in his own exposition, in order to
provide an intuitive check on results to be obtained in a more
formal way later on.

These three can best be expressed in three kinds of "formula"
which I shall call the "to say" formula, the "in saying" formula,
and the "hereby" formula. The first exhibits the very notion of

[4] J. R. Ross offers good reasons to think that some performative verb,
and the *I*, is actually present even in the deep-structure of simple declarative sentences when they occur in actual use ("On Declarative Sentences,"
in R. Jacobs and P. Rosenbaum, ed., *Readings in Transformational Grammar*).

a "performative" utterance (i.e., to say something is to do something); for example,

> To say (in the appropriate circumstances) "I *promise* to pay you $5.00" is to *promise* to pay somebody $5.00.

In an implicit case:

> To say (in the appropriate circumstances) "The bull is charging" is to *warn* somebody that the bull is charging.

The "in saying" formula is equally central to the notion of an "in-locutionary" act (i.e., doing something in saying something); for example:

> In saying that the bull was charging he *warned* his companion.

Finally, the possibility of adjoining the adverb *hereby* to the first person singular present indicative active occurrence of a performative verb gives us the "hereby" formula; for example:

> I hereby *promise* to pay you $5.00.

In spite of the intuitive aid these formulae provide for the understanding of what illocutionary acts are, and how performative verbs function, Austin's own discussion shows that they cannot be relied upon, severally or jointly, to form a criterion for the recognition of performative verbs. (But little imagination is required to make obviously undesirable verbs fit into these formulae, or to find some performatives which would not enter them for some reason or other.) Moreover, from a linguistic point of view, these formulae, even in a suitably generalized form, are *ad hoc* creations which do not tie in with the system of grammar, and which, accordingly, shed no light on the deeper syntactical function of performative verbs. Hence Austin's persistent quest for a truly "grammatical" criterion.

3. Indeed, he seems to find one. He notices that it is the first person singular form of the present perfect (i.e., nonprogressive) tense of the performative verb that carries the illocutionary force, and, consequently, is a true present in the sense of, roughly, indicating what happens at the moment of the utterance, whereas the progressive tense hardly occurs at all. This is in marked contrast with most other verbs: *I am smoking*, for instance, is the usual form of reporting my concurrent smoking; *I smoke* is used to admit a disreputable habit. Hence the possibility of saying *I smoke but I am not smoking now. I promise to pay on time*, on the other hand, is normally used to make a promise (which is made, *ipso dicto*, at that moment) and does not say anything about the speaker's habit of promising. The same thing holds of other typical performatives; think of *I warn, I order, I sentence, I name*, and so forth. The progressive tense is quite alien to these verbs, except for some such colloquial emphatic uses as *I am warning you*.[5] Having found this interesting and important feature, Austin then proceeds to use "the simple test (with caution) of the first person present indicative active form" in going through the dictionary to hunt for performatives.[6]

Is this test good enough? The obvious answer is that it is not. There are entire families of clearly nonperformative verbs that share the same preference for the present perfect even in the first person singular—for example, the intuitive group of verbs

---

[5] Notice that such a sentence usually occurs following the warning itself. *I am warning you* is not a warning; it is a reminder of a warning.
[6] *How to Do Things with Words*, p. 149.

On Saying Something

that traditionally have been called "propositional attitude" verbs: *believe, know, understand, doubt, remember, expect, intend,* and the like. Then there are other, shall we say, "attitude" verbs, like *love, hate, prefer, detest,* and so forth. Not even the best intentions in the world can make these performatives: they certainly do not fit into the formulae discussed above; yet they pass the present perfect test with no trouble, and show the same reluctance toward the progressive form as the genuine performatives. Thus it is not surprising that Austin, employing this supposed criterion, comes to wonder about *know, believe,* and *doubt,*[7] and that such verbs as *value, understand, envisage, favor, resent, overlook, intend* and *regard* turn up unquestioned in his final list. Some of these may have performative uses now and then, but by and large they show a much greater resemblance to the verbs of propositional (or other) attitudes. To anticipate: they are "thinking" verbs rather than "saying" verbs.

4. The fact that the alleged criterion lets in not just a few unimportant or borderline items, but large families of very common verbs that are not performatives, signals the breakdown of that criterion. Yet, I think, Austin's intuition that performative verbs are akin to propositional attitude verbs spurs us in the right direction. The obvious similarity between these two groups is the following: both kinds normally take, or at least can take, a noun clause rather than a simple noun for verb-object. We know, believe, or think *that something is the case,* we doubt or wonder *whether something is the case,* and we may remember *what we did yesterday.* In a similar way, I may state, predict, or warn you *that something is going to happen,* I may promise *to do something,* and I may apologize *for having done something.*

[7] *Ibid.,* pp. 90, 161.

11

Res Cogitans

After all, the very name, propositional attitude, suggests that the objects of those verbs are not simple nouns but sentences or propositions. As for performative verbs, we recall that they are like labels attached not to nouns but to utterances to mark their illocutionary force. To use another simile, the performative verb is like a frame or container in which an utterance is enclosed and offered in a particular way. It appears, then, that both performatives and verbs like *know, believe,* and *doubt* belong to the same genus of container verbs, verbs, that is, the object of which is a noun-clause or, in modern terminology, a sentence nominalization of a certain type.[8] Thus it is not surprising that they share an added feature, namely, the preference for the present perfect tense. Austin recognized a characteristic of the genus to which the performatives belong, but, owing to his lack of attention to the form of the appropriate verb-object, failed to recognize the genus itself, not to speak of the specific difference that separates the performatives from the other branches of the same genus.

Austin leads us to the gates of the Promised Land, but he himself does not enter. It is up to us to continue the journey, first looking at the performatives in this new perspective and then trying to find the real criteria that set them apart. As we are going to see, this study will yield two unexpected by-products. First, a natural subdivision of the class of performatives: a result which will vindicate Austin's own intuition in the grouping of illocutionary forces. And, second—a still more important gain— by viewing the performatives in the natural context of other "propositional" verbs, we will obtain the first glimpse of the true relation of speech and thought.

---

[8] See R. B. Lees, *The Grammar of English Nominalizations,* my *Adjectives and Nominalizations,* and my *Linguistics in Philosophy,* Ch. 5.

12

On Saying Something

5.   Performatives are container verbs of a certain kind. In order
to illustrate this point in some detail, I shall give a list of utterances, the production of which, provided it is "happy" in Austin's sense (i.e., not affected by some "infelicities" of context
and circumstance), normally amounts to the performance of an
illocutionary act. After each utterance I shall add the sentence
from which the particular verb-object has been derived by the
nominalizing transformation. In this list I purposely include
examples from the whole range of illocutionary acts.

(1)   I suggest that Joe committed the crime
(1a) Joe committed the crime
(2)   I deny having seen the victim
(2a) I have seen the victim
(3)   I call it murder
(3a) It is murder
(4)   I urge you to proceed
(4a) You should proceed
(5)   I appoint you to the presidency
(5a) You shall become the president
(6)   I promise to pay on time
(6a) I shall pay on time
(7)   I apologize for having offended you
(7a) I have offended you.

The morphological details of the nominalizations appearing
in this list will be discussed in due course. For the time being
I merely call attention to the fact that nominalizations of this
kind are to be distinguished from those of another sort, which
correspond to entirely different container verbs. Some examples:

I am watching the sunset
I am listening to his singing

I am observing the passage of Venus
I am imitating his walk.

Elsewhere, I have described in in great detail the differences between these two kinds of nominalization.[9] By way of a rough summary, one can say that the product of the former kind, which I called the "imperfect" nominal, expresses a proposition, whereas the product of this latter kind, called the "perfect" nominal, denotes an event, process, or action. Since these things, unlike propositions, are temporal entities, which occur, go on, or take place somewhere in the world, it is not surprising to find "perceptual" container verbs in the list just given, and these occurring in the progressive tense, indicating temporal succession. The simple present, on the other hand, neatly corresponds to the atemporal nature of propositions.

Nevertheless it is exactly a temporal aspect that will split the class of propositional verbs into performatives and verbs of propositional attitudes, a feature which has escaped Austin's grammar. It is quite clear that whereas the simple present tense, in the case of a performative, singles out the moment at which the illocutionary act occurs, in the case of a propositional attitude verb the same tense does not indicate a unique moment, but an indefinite time-span which includes the moment of the utterance. To use the terminology I introduced in an earlier work, performatives are achievement verbs, but propositional attitude verbs are state verbs according to their time-schema.[10] *When (at what moment) did you promise such and such?* and *For how long did you believe such and such?* are the proper questions, and *At 5 p.m.* and *For a year or so*, respectively, the appropriate answers, and not the other way around. Again, compare *I still believe* with *I still promise*. The first phrase

---

[9] *Linguistics in Philosophy*, Ch. 5.   [10] *Ibid.*, Ch. 4.

needs no explanation; the second does. It might mean that I have not withdrawn my promise, or that I am still willing to promise, but certainly not that my promising has not yet come to an end.

This difference in their time-schema would be sufficient to distinguish thinking words from saying words, were it not for the fact that there are some propositional verbs with the achievement schema which are nevertheless obviously words of thought and not of saying. *Decide, realize, discover, identify, recognize,* and the like are achievement verbs, yet, typically, are not performatives. Their behavior with respect to the present tense, however, is very different from that of the performatives. With a performative, the first person singular present form is the most characteristic, and indeed the primary occurrence. Members of the *decide*-group, on the contrary, do not occur in this form except when accompanied by grammatical adjuncts indicating general scope. There is nothing missing in such a sentence as *I promise to pay on time* or *I warn you that the bull is going to charge.* On the other hand, the sentence **I decide to go home,* or **I discover the correct method,* is distinctly deviant. *I decide* and *I discover* are only acceptable in such contexts as *I always decide on the spur of the moment* or *I never discover anything without hard work.* This feature is not so obvious with the other three verbs just listed. Looking closer we realize, however, that in case they are acceptable in the simple present without a modifier indicating general scope, they occur as a performative or as a propositional attitude verb. *Realize,* for example, appears in the role of a propositional attitude verb in the context *I realize that such and such is the case.* *Identify* and *recognize,* on the other hand, may function as performatives: think of *I hereby identify the accused as the man who . . .* or *I hereby recognize the deputy as the representative of. . . .*

To conclude, performatives belong to the genus of propositional verbs, that is, container verbs corresponding to imperfect nominals, all of which show the symptomatic reluctance toward the progressive form. This genus, however, splits into three main species: (a) performatives, with achievement time-schema and unmodified first person singular present occurrence; (b) the *decide*-group, with the same time-schema but no such present occurrence; (c) propositional attitude verbs with the state time-schema. For the sake of simplicity I shall refer to the last two classes as verbs of mental act and verbs of mental state.

As we see, the correction of Austin's criterion has led us to the recognition of two closely related classes. This relationship will assume great importance later on. Presently, however, I shall discuss the performatives themselves in some detail. In doing this I am going to follow a generative approach by putting, as it were, our new criteria to work. First I shall enumerate the main types of structure in which imperfect nominals occur; then select the verbs that correspond to each type; and finally weed out state verbs and those achievement verbs that have no unqualified first person present. The residue will be the list of performatives already classified according to structural principles. The fact that these subclasses substantially mirror Austin's own intuitive subdivisions will show not only his acumen, but the correctness and fertility of our improved criteria.

In the following sections I shall restrict myself to the listing of the performative verbs. The rest, the ones I have weeded out in the process, will be taken up in the next chapter.

6. The simplest, and indeed paradigm form of propositional object is the *that*-clause. The class of performatives that normally take such an object corresponds to Austin's "expositives." This is a very large class comprising many obvious subdivisions,

the exact delineation of which, however, would require much
more detail than I can here afford to give. Accordingly I shall
rely on intuition in giving these subclasses. For my own con-
solation, I appeal to intuition one step later than Austin.[11]

I begin with the "strong" declaratives: *state, declare, assert,
affirm, claim, contend, maintain,* and *insist.* The next three,
guess, submit, and *suggest,* represent a somewhat weaker com-
mitment. Then there are some special groups: *agree, disagree,
concede,* and *deny* give one's reaction to someone else's word;
report, testify, admit, confess, and *predict* are temporally marked,
explicitly invoking the past or the future; *postulate, argue,* and
conclude operate in a logical context; finally, the obligatory
direct object (*you* in the performative case) clearly sets apart
the following five: *tell, assure, inform, remind,* and *warn.*

The *that*-clause is often replaced by such variants as the ones
in

> I confess having seen her
> I admit his superiority
> I warn you of his dishonesty.

Yet the *that*-form is always available and remains typical. In a
similar way, examples like

> He predicted the war
> He denied her allegation
> He warned me of the bull

[11] Some very recent work by C. J. Fillmore promises a more accurate
subclassification of the whole performative domain by exposing the various
presuppositions behind the use of these verbs (see Bibliography). What,
for example, does *insist* presuppose, which *state* does not? Obviously, things
like past assertion of the same thing, persistent challenge, etc. These are,
admittedly, *minutiae,* but if science finds it worth while to describe thou-
sands of bugs in a thousand and one details, why should the particulars of
our mental habitat deserve less patience or devotion?

require but little sophistication to be recognized as deletion-products of sentences like

> He predicted (that) the war (would come)
> He denied (that *p*, which) she alleged
> He warned me (that) the bull (was dangerous).

Again, *wh*-morphemes may replace some elements in the nominalized sentence leading to such results as

> He stated what he found
> She told us where he went

and so forth.[12] The grammatical moves behind such derivative surface forms are very common and by this time fairly well known. Thus I shall not pay particular attention to such "standard" deviations, unless they are peculiar to a given structure.

Another point, too, is worth mentioning at least once. Some of the verbs which have an expositive role may have other uses as well. *Warn* and *tell*, for instance, can also be followed by the structure which, as we are going to see, defines Austin's "exercitives"; for example:

> I tell you to leave the premises
> I warn you not to enter the room.

Some other expositives reach beyond the performative domain altogether: one can submit oneself to one's enemy, and the porter can admit the latecomers. These are but the first exam-

---

12 Interestingly enough, the *wh*-forms cannot occur performatively except in such replies as *I agree with what you said*. The sentence *I predict what will happen* is deviant if not actually followed by a prediction. This alone is sufficient to show that *know* is not a performative: *I know what is going to happen* is a knowledge claim even if the speaker does not go on to reveal what he knows. More about this in Chapter V.

ples of many performatives that, as it were, play for more than one club, or even outside the league. This fact, however, does not blunt the distinction between the clubs or the leagues. (See Appendix I.)

7. Austin's "verdictives" are similar to the previous class, except for the fact that the sentence which gets nominalized contains the copula rather than some other verb. This leads to another structure, which obligatorily replaces the *that*-clause: the subject of the nominalized sentence becomes the direct object of the performative and the copula gets deleted or replaced by *as* (occasionally by *to be*). Some examples:

> I *call* it murder
> I *rank* him second
> I *classify* the piece (as) a novel.

This is much smaller class. Yet some subdivisions clearly emerge. First of all, there is a group that measures the objects in question as it were on a scale: *rank, grade, place* (e.g. horses after a race), *appraise*, and *rate*. A broader perspective corresponds to *call, describe, characterize, diagnose, classify, define*, and *distinguish*. With this last verb the nominalized sentence seems to be negative: *I distinguish X from Y* contains X *is not* Y. The last group suggests legal context: *plead, rule*, and *find*. *Plead* shows an interesting peculiarity: the identity of subject between the performative and the nominalized sentence permits the contraction found in *I plead guilty*.

8. In the class of "commissives" two new elements enter the picture: a noun-sharing between the subject of the performative and the subject of the nominalized sentence, and an auxiliary

(*shall* or *will*) in the latter sentence. *Promise* belongs to this class:

I promise (you) to pay on time

which codes the full form:

I promise (you) that *I shall* pay on time.

Some other commissives are *undertake, covenant, contract, pledge, guarantee, vow, swear,* and the negatives *refuse* and *decline.* Notice that one can guarantee the future conduct or quality of things other than oneself: *We guarantee the car to last.* . . . This looks like an "exercitive" (see below), but a more careful analysis would reveal something like *We guarantee to recompense you if the car does not last* . . . in the background.

9. There are two structures corresponding to Austin's "exercitives." The first, for which I shall retain the name, is shown in such sentences as

I *order* you to proceed
I *advise* you to remain silent.

The infinitive construction in the nominal once more conceals an auxiliary (in this case the "subjunctive equivalent" *should*), and the subject of the nominalized sentence again appears as the direct object of the performative. This, at least in the performative occurrence, is almost always *you.* Spelled out in full:

I order *you* that *you should* proceed
I advise *you* that *you* (*should*) remain silent.

This construction picks out a fairly large class of performatives; a subdivision may help us to see their variety. *Order, com-*

mand, demand (*of* or *from*) and the ambivalent *tell* (see section 6, above) are more categorical than *request, ask, urge, counsel,* and *advise;* these, in turn, are stronger than *permit* and *allow.* Again, whereas *entreat, pray, beseech,* and *beg* appeal to one's kindness, *dare* and *challenge* provoke one's courage. *Forbid* and *prohibit* have a negative sense by themselves, but the bifurcating *warn* (see section 6) requires a subsequent negation: consider *I forbid you to* . . . versus *I warn you not to.* . . . In this last case what probably happens is that an unspecified threat is deleted: the explicit form would be something like *I warn you that I shall* . . . (or *it will* . . .) *if you.* . . .[13]

10. The next group, which Austin failed to distinguish from the exercitives, shows some similarity both to these and to the verdictives. The subject of the nominalized sentence once again appears as the direct object of the performative. As with the verdictives, the verb-phrase of that sentence contains a copulative verb; only here it is more likely to be *become* than *be.* Moreover, as with the exercitives, it is affected by the subjunctive or an equivalent modal. But there is a new feature too: if we want to give the full, uncontracted form of the elements entering the construction we feel that the connective *so that* rather than simply *that* should be used. In an example, the derivation goes as follows:

> I appoint *you* so that *you* (*shall*) *be*(*come*) the president
> I appoint you to be(come) the president
> I appoint you to the presidency.

I shall call the performatives fitting into this slot "operatives." Many members of this very large class conform to the given

[13] Another way of cutting the pie would involve the notion of presupposed authority. *Order, command, permit, allow, forbid,* and *prohibit,* but not the rest, seem to require some authority in the speaker.

pattern without hitch. They are the ones that are used to change the status of persons (or other things) in a positive sense: *recommend, nominate, appoint, name, elect, hire, admit,* and *promote* (primarily persons); *propose, dedicate, proclaim, assign, consign,* and *relegate* (primarily things). With such negative verbs as *degrade, demote, dismiss, fire,* and *suspend,* the pattern has to be stretched. Some construction like

I demote you so that you shall cease to be . . .

must be at the source.

The *so that* instead of *that* is the very soul of an operative utterance. It marks its "efficiency": in issuing an operative I say something and the social, ritual, or legal effect *ipso dicto* takes place. Compare this with the verdictives. They are used to establish, albeit by a qualified speaker, what is the case; the operatives determine what shall be. Therefore the former speech acts remain, in a sense, in the domain of truth and falsity. Even in the highly ritualistic cases of placing (e.g., horses after the race) or grading (say, students), the assumption remains that these acts "truly" describe or evaluate the performance. This, obviously, is not the case with the operatives. They do not describe or evaluate a given situation: they create a new one. Hence *become* (or *cease to be*) rather than *is* in the typical matrix.

In this perspective we can discern whole families of additional operatives: *arrest, sentence, condemn, fine,* and *appeal* in the legal sphere; *baptize, confirm, ordain, absolve, excommunicate,* and *canonize* in the religious, *knight* in the feudal domain; perhaps also *offer, give, grant, surrender, accept, refuse,* and *reject,* as well as *greet, salute,* and *welcome.* With some of these the general pattern will work only in a seemingly trivial sense. Consider *arrest* and *baptize:*

On Saying Something

    I arrest you so that you shall be(come) arrested
    I baptize you so that you shall be(come) baptized.

This seems to be a travesty of a derivation. For, after all, what prevents one from claiming that, say, behind *I kick you*, there must be something like

    I kick you so that you shall be kicked?

This is a serious matter, for if this objection holds up, then our claim that all performatives are propositional verbs goes by the board. Where is the "proposition" in the object of *I arrest you*?

To discuss this problem here would mean a long and distracting digression; it is treated in full in Appendix II.

11. The "behabitives" are an easier matter. They can be collected by using the pattern exhibited by, say,

    I thank you for having helped me
    I apologize for having hurt you.

Obviously there is a noun-sharing here between the subject of the contained sentence and either the direct object (as with *thank*) or the subject (as with *apologize*) of the performative. The contained sentence, however, does not have a modal verb, but a verb usually in the past tense. The verb-phrase of this sentence is brought in by means of a preposition: *for, upon,* or *against*. The variety of prepositions suggests a subclassification. The favorable *thank, praise,* and *command* and the unfavorable *apologize, censure,* and *pardon* require *for; congratulate, felicitate, and compliment* lean toward *upon; protest,* finally, calls for *against. Protest,* incidentally, is followed by a slightly different structure.

12. A small but important class of performatives must be added to this list. The verbs *ask, question,* and *inquire* are normally followed by what grammarians call an "indirect question." This is nothing but a nominal formed out of a sentence by either prefixing *whether* or by replacing a noun or adverbial phrase by the appropriate *wh*-word: *who, what, when, where, why, how,* etc. Examples:

> I question whether he has succeeded
> I ask (you) how he did it.

These, naturally, can be called "interrogatives."

13. By way of summary, the results of our discussion are here set out formally. My purpose in doing this is not merely to show the coherence of the preceding classification, but also to prepare the way for a parallel classification to be made in the next chapter. Given the previous discussion, the symbolism will speak for itself.

Expositives:
$N_i V_{ep} [N V +]$ $\longrightarrow N_i V_{ep}$ *that* $N V +$

Verdictives:
$N_i V_{vd} [N_j$ *is* $N_k/A]$ $\longrightarrow N_i V_{vd} N_j$ *(as)* N_k/A

Commissives:
$N_i V_{cm} [N_i \bmod(V +)]$ $\longrightarrow N_i V_{cm}$ *to* $V +$

Exercitives:
$N_i V_{ee} [N_j \bmod(V +)]$ $\longrightarrow N_i V_{ee} N_j$ *to* $V +$

Operatives:
$N_i V_{op} [N_j$ *becomes* $N_k]$ $\longrightarrow N_i V_{op} N_j$ *to be(come)* N_k
or, from Appendix II:
$N_i C [N_j$ *becomes* $W]$ $\longrightarrow N_i V_{op_w} N_j$

On Saying Something

Behavitives:

$$N_i V_{bh} [N_j past(V +)] \longrightarrow N_i V_{bh} N_j P nom (past (V+))$$

Interrogatives:

$$N_i V_{ir} [N V +] \longrightarrow N_i V_{ir} \text{ wh-nom} (N V +)$$

14. Finally, a few words about the verb *say*. It often has performative uses: *I say* can introduce statements, orders, promises, apologies, and what not. Again, the question *What did he say?* may be answered by alluding to all sorts of speech-acts: *He stated that . . . , He promised to . . . , He ordered you to . . . , He apologized . . . , He asked me whether . . . ,* and so forth. It appears, therefore, that *say* is a sort of general performative. The same thing, of course, can also be inferred from its occurrence in the first two Austinian "formulae" given above. These facts are more than enough to show that Austin's discussion, and our own, of illocutionary acts indeed contribute to the analysis of the concept of saying something. To perform an illocutionary act is to say something in the full sense of the word.

Yet this is not the whole story of saying. The same verb can be used in another sense too: one can say words, phrases, and sentences, one can say tongue twisters, rhymes, and rigmaroles, in one's own tongue or in a language otherwise unknown; even parrots and talking dolls can "say" many things in this sense of the word. Yet, obviously, none of these "sayings" will carry an illocutionary force. This weak sense of saying is roughly equivalent to uttering, mouthing, or pronouncing.

Now it is important to realize that these two levels of saying things are radically different. An illocutionary act is not a mere mouthing of a sentence in a certain situation. The circumstances may be right and the sentence well formed, the *I* prefixed and the performative verb in its due place—nevertheless, no illocutionary act will be performed if, for one thing, the speaker does not understand what he is saying, or, for another, he does not intend to perform such an act, that is, does not intend his audience to take him to be performing one. No matter what the parrot says, it will not make a statement, issue an order, or give a promise; no matter with how serious a mien the child pronounces "Omnia sunt vanitas," he will not say that all things are vanity if he does not know Latin at all; and no matter how much invective I heap upon you, you have no reason to take offence, though you might think you have, if I am but engaged, sincerely from my part yet unbeknownst to you, in rehearsing a play.

Saying in the weak sense falls far short of saying in the full sense; one must understand what one says and one must mean what one says. In this chapter we have surveyed the costumes for the performance, not the actors; we have examined the frames, not the contents.

III

Thoughts

1.   Performatives, as we have seen in the previous chapter, are but one species of the genus of propositional verbs. We have found two other groups, which I called verbs of mental act and verbs of mental state. The former, exemplified by *decide*, are achievement verbs like the performatives, but, unlike them, they lack the unqualified present occurrence. The latter, exemplified by *believe*, are easily distinguished from either of the previous classes by their state time-schema.

In this chapter I shall collect these verbs, which were systematically set aside in compiling the catalogue of performatives, and then show that, just as the performatives spell out the various ways of saying something, these verbs display the possible forms of thought. Moreover, as the analogy between the basic frames of speech and thought emerges, together with the identity of their possible content, we will grasp the principles required for the solution of the problems mentioned at the end of the preceding chapter. We are going to realize, with increasing clarity as we go on, the truth and the philosophical importance of the commonsense view that speech is essentially the expression of thought.

The tactical steps to be taken in classifying our two groups of verbs are determined by our previous work with the performatives. With respect to each main type of propositional verb-object, we shall ask the question: are there any verbs taking such an object that conform to the tense-criteria, first of mental-act verbs and second of mental-state verbs? Following Austin's example I shall give a name to each of the non-empty classes thus obtained.

A word of caution: as there were "moonlighting" performatives, there will be two-faced, or even many-faced, verbs in our present domain. As we are going to see, there is a particularly strong tendency to use some original performatives in an extended sense—that is, to denote not a speech-act, but a mental act or even state. Owing to the richness of the performative vocabulary, there is a great temptation to borrow some of its items for a different, yet closely related use. We shall encounter some obvious examples of such "leakage" soon enough.

2. What, then, are the mental-act verbs corresponding to the *that*-clause? There are a few "pure" items: *find out, discover, learn, infer, deduce,* and *establish.* These have no performative occurrence and cannot take on the state-schema: **I discover that . . . , *I still deduce that. . . .* Others, such as *notice, gather, understand, realize,* and the temporally marked *recollect,* display some symptoms of the state-occurrence: *I notice that . . . , I understand that . . . , I realize that . . . ,* but hardly **I still realize that . . . , *Since when do you understand that . . . ,* and so forth. *Guess* and *conclude,* on the other hand, are probably borrowed performatives. One can guess or conclude something not only in words, but also without saying anything. This possibility, of course, indicates an extension

Thoughts

beyond the performative domain. Finally, I mention the multifarious *see*, since one of its uses obviously belongs here, being a near synonym to *realize*. . . . I shall call this class "apprehensives."

The corresponding mental-state verbs come in a fair variety. The most typical group once more displays the familiar gamut of "firmness" going from the rather negative *doubt*, through the weak *suspect, surmise, imagine, assume*, and *suppose*, through the stronger *think, believe*, and *hold*, up to the categorical, and all important, *know*. Needless to say that many of these verbs bifurcate: think of holding candles, assuming duties, and imagining pink rats. The etymology behind these ambivalences is interesting, but we can do without it at this point. There is another group with temporal connotations: *remember, recall, expect, anticipate*, and the emotively tinged *hope* and *fear*. Then, as we recall, there is some leakage from the apprehensives (*realize*, etc.) and some from the performatives: one can maintain things, agree or disagree with people in one's heart as well as in speech. This group of verbs I call "putatives."

3. Turning to the "mental" verbs corresponding to the verdictives, we find but a few achievement verbs: *recognize* and *identify*, on the one hand, and *estimate* and *judge*, on the other, seem to be the natives of this domain, although they all show a tendency to appear in the performative garb now and then. Here, for once, the "leakage" seems to go the other way. The structural similarity to the verdictives is obvious:

> I recognized the man as the one who . . .
> I estimated its value to be . . .
> I judged him incompetent.

The fact that, say, *recognize* might occur in the present tense, even in a nonperformative way, does not change the picture.

Res Cogitans

I still recognize him is an ellipsis for *I still can recognize him;* to be able to recognize is, of course, a state. The point is, however, that the *can* version is out of place with respect to a real state verb, for example *regard. I regard him as a coward* is not an ellipsis for *I can regard him as a coward.* To this small class I give a trivial name: "recognitives."

There is a much greater variety in the state equivalents of verdictives. Even the two main semantic groups of the verdictives have their shadows here: *deem, esteem, value,* and, perhaps, *appreciate* assess worth, whereas *take, consider, regard, look upon,* and *see* require a broader semantic frame. The last three (perhaps four) are borrowed from the perceptual domain, yet they transcend it in the present frame, as in *I see it as a crime.* So, of course, does *take* transcend the physical domain in, say, *We take it to be self-evident.* . . . I christen this group "assessives."

4. The commissives, too, have their cognate families. On the achievement side we find our old paradigm *decide* together with *resolve, choose,* and *elect.* As you promise or vow to do something, you decide, resolve, choose, or elect to do something. To name these few verbs I resort to the trivial once more and suggest "resolutives."

There is no difficulty in naming the next class, which contains the state equivalents of commissives. It comes naturally to call this rich and important class "conatives." Intuitively, they fall into two groups; whereas *want, intend, plan, mean,* and *contemplate* (*to do something,* of course) do not connote emotions, *wish, aspire, desire, long, hope,* and *covet* clearly do. I am not sure about *prefer* in this respect. The "emotional" group is mainly concerned with becoming something or coming to have something; consequently *be* or *have* are often redundant in the verb object. Hence abbreviated surface forms like

Thoughts

He aspires the presidency
He longs for adulation
He covets Joe's wife.

Otherwise, the structural similarity between the commissives and resolutives is too obvious to waste words on.

5. To our initial dismay, we find the classes corresponding to the exercitives and operatives almost empty. This stands to reason, however. Exercitives are used, roughly, to cause other people to do something, whereas operatives bring about certain (institutional, legal, or religious) results *ipso dicto*. Unvoiced thoughts, however, cannot move other people; nor can they be effective in the institutional sphere.

One can wish, of course, that other people do certain things, and one can decide to effect certain institutional changes in one's power. If we do such things, we naturally use the resolutive or conative vocabulary to express it (albeit with a suitably adjusted structure); for example,

I want him to go home
I chose him to do the job.

A few originals, namely *select, pick* and *design*, fit into the same structure. In addition, one might resort to metaphorical phrases like *I have him in mind to* (or *for*). . . . Think of the Pope actually creating a cardinal *"in pectore."* Fortunately such real exercitive thinking is the privilege of the exalted few.

6. Are there mental-act verbs sharing the syntactical slot inhabited by the behabitives? I can think of two: *forgive* and *condone*. There are not many state verbs either: we have the favorable *approve of* and *sympathize with* and the unfavorable *blame, resent, disapprove of*, and *regret*. Some of these, notably *condone* and *sympathize*, show slight deviations from the be-

habitive paradigm. *Regret,* like the behabitive *apologize,* reflects upon the speaker's own past actions. To keep up the naming game I shall call the first small class "remissives" and the second "emotives."

7. Finally, the interrogatives have the lone "inquisitive," *wonder,* for a counterpart. This, of course, is a state verb.

8. In order to recapitulate the results of our long, and perhaps tedious, effort at classifying propositional verbs, I shall display them in a series of synoptic tables. The notation will speak for itself. Since the structures given are applicable beyond the performative domain, I shall omit the subscripts marking the propositional verbs. The arrows indicate the direction of "leakage" between the categories. Needless to say that the semantic subclassification is largely intuitive, consequently by no means final and, probably, often wrong. Nevertheless the presence of these semantic factors, and their scope embracing words of speech and thought alike, are certain and are instructive. Owing to the lack of parallelism, I shall omit the commissives and the exercitives.

(a) N_i V *that* N V +

Expositives	Apprehensives	Putatives
state	find out	know
declare	discover	hold
assert	notice	think
affirm	see $\longrightarrow$	believe
claim	realize	
contend		
maintain $\longrightarrow$		
insist		

Thoughts

Expositives	Apprehensives	Putatives
agree ———→		
concede		

disagree ———→		
deny		

postulate	infer	
argue	deduce	
conclude ———→	establish	

tell	learn	
assure	gather ———→	
inform	understand ———→	
remind		
warn		

report	recollect	remember
testify	←———	recall
admit		
confess		

predict		expect
		anticipate
		hope
		fear

guess ———→		suspect
submit	←———	surmise
suggest		imagine
	←———	assume
		suppose
		doubt

(b) N V N (*as*) N/A

Verdictives		Recognitives		Assessives
rank	←——	estimate		deem
grade	←——	judge	←——	esteem
place			←——	value
appraise				appreciate
rate				

call	←——	recognize	←——	take
describe	←——	identify		consider
characterize				regard
diagnose ——→				look upon
classify ——→			←——	see
define				
distinguish ——→				

plead
rule
find ——→

(c) N V *to* V +

Commissives		Resolutives	Conatives
promise	←——	decide	want
undertake		resolve	intend
covenant	←——	choose	plan
contract		elect	mean
pledge			contemplate
guarantee			prefer
vow			
swear			

Thoughts

Commissives	Resolutives	Conatives
refuse decline		
		wish aspire desire long covet

(d) N V N P nom(past(V +))

Behabitives	Remissives	Emotives
thank praise commend		⟵ approve of
congratulate felicitate compliment		sympathize
censure protest		⟵ blame ⟵ disapprove of resent
pardon ⟵	forgive condone ⟶	
apologize		regret

Res Cogitans

(e) N V wh-nom(N V +)

Interrogatives	Inquisitives
ask	wonder
question	
inquire	

9. Thus surveyed, the domain of propositional verbs reveals a staggering perspective: the almost universal identity of the objects of speech and thought. For—to show off some fruits of our hard-earned erudition—the same things that can be asserted, suggested, or denied in words, can be realized, and understood, believed, suspected, or doubted in thought; things regarded, considered, looked upon, and recognized to be such and such in thought, can also be characterized, described, and defined in the same way in words; what one may wish, want, intend, or decide to do in thought, one also can promise, vow, or pledge to do in words; the same things that are worthy of blame, approval, resentment, or forgiveness in thought, deserve to be censured, praised, objected to, and pardoned in words; finally what one wonders about in thought, one can ask about in speech. To put it briefly: you can say whatever you think, and you can think *almost* whatever you can say. This last qualification is necessary in view of the fact that there are two performative fields, those of the exercitives and the operatives, that do not have a direct counterpart in the mental domain. Indirectly, of course, *via* the necessary intention to perform these speech acts, even these fields are related to thought.

Indeed, the use of the very word *thought* is commonly extended to cover what has been said or written, albeit with the exception of exercitive and operative speech. It does not take mind-reading to acquaint oneself with somebody else's thought;

36

ordinary reading or listening is enough; only honesty is required in the writer and understanding in the reader. The *Little Red Book* contains Chairman Mao's thought; yet it is but a book of quotations: it records the statements he made, the promises he gave, the proposals he issued, the challenges he hurled, the praises he offered to his friends, and the condemnations he heaped upon his foes. If he was sincere, these are his thoughts.

For, I repeat, honesty is required: people can lie, dissimulate their intentions, and praise and blame with the tongue but not the heart. What is said, if said with meaning and not merely parrotwise, is a thought, but it may not be the real thought of the speaker. There are thoughts not revealed, not expressed, not given voice; saying and thinking are not the same thing.

10. What, then, is the difference? Is it merely that speech is a noisy form of thinking, and thinking is a silent way of talking to oneself? That the difference is much less trivial can be gathered from the fact that most thinking verbs are state verbs, whereas the performatives are one and all achievement verbs. But there is another, much more illuminating way of approaching the problem. There is a common device of reverbalizing a nominalized verb by using an *ad hoc* auxiliary. Instead of saying *I kicked*, I can say *I gave a kick*; instead of *I looked*, *I took a look*, and so on. The same move is possible in regard to most propositional verbs. One speaks of giving a promise, holding a belief, or arriving at a decision. The auxiliaries are more or less metaphorical, but this is not a reason for disdaining their aid. For, as we are going to see, the consideration of these auxiliaries casts an extraordinary light on the relation between a person and a proposition, be it the relation of saying or thinking. In any case, we are still in a preparatory stage, putting our minds into the correct frame to discuss the relation of speech and

thought with due philosophical rigor, which will be the task of the next chapter.

To begin with the performatives, the most common auxiliaries are *make, give,* and particularly *issue.* One makes a statement, gives a promise, and issues a denial. There are a number of offbeat forms: one offers a proposal, hurls a challenge, pronounces a verdict, hands down a decision, and sounds a warning. The verb *issue* is the most typical: it fits almost all the performatives. This is no surprise; after all, these verbs, as Austin noted, are verbs of issuance: the proposition in question is issued, pronounced (*pro-nuntio*), given out.

The verbs of thinking call for a totally different set of auxiliaries. With respect to the state verbs, *have* is the most common: one has beliefs, opinions, suspicions, desires, regrets, and what not. The offbeat auxiliaries add color to the picture. Take *belief:* like a child, it is conceived, adopted, or embraced; it is nurtured, held, cherished, and entertained; or, if it appears misbegotten, it may be abandoned or given up. The same is true, with less variety, of suspicions, intentions, resentments, and the like. This image is *toto coelo* different from the one evoked by the set corresponding to the performatives; there is no issuance here, the objects of these states being "in" or "with" the person, "held" in one way or another. Moreover, they can be hidden, concealed, or, on the other hand, shown, manifested, expressed, or given voice. What we hold (for a time) in a mental state, we can issue (at a time) in an illocutionary act.

Mental-act verbs share *make* with some performatives: we make decisions, identifications, choices, and so on, just as we make statements, proposals, declarations, and the like. *Make* seems to mark achievement verbs in this domain. Yet the difference remains between the two kinds. Statements, proposals, or declarations can also be issued, which is not true of iden-

Thoughts

tifications or choices. As for decisions, they can be issued. But obviously, *decide*, in that case, functions as a performative; the counterexample, in fact, works for us. The less standard auxiliaries, such as *reach* (a decision) and *arrive at* (a realization), illustrate the achievement aspect of these verbs. Whereas a mental state is like having or possessing something, a mental act is often like finding or getting hold of something, or, in other cases, like reaching a goal.[1]

The total import of the emerging picture is clear enough. Man lives in two environments, in two worlds: as a "body," an "extended thing," he is among objects and events in the physical, spatiotemporal universe; as a "mind," a "thinking thing," he lives and communes with objects of a different kind, which he also perceives, acquires, holds, and offers in various ways to other citizens of this world, to other minds.

11. It will be objected that I misrepresent here the concept of thinking; that by focusing exclusively on the sense of the word *thought* which denotes the content or product of the mental processes I ignore these processes themselves or, worse, that by capitalizing on a quirk of the vernacular, I create the impression that by discussing thought in this sense I have exhausted the topic of thinking altogether. "What you are doing"—an opponent might argue—"is a typical case of a process-product confusion; it is like suggesting that the word *building* denotes only an edifice, forgetting the other sense, which denotes the activity

---

[1] It is rather instructive to try the verb *try* (and its cognates, *succeed* and *fail*) on performatives and mental verbs. Compare, for instance, *He tried to state (deny, tell)* . . . and *He tried to believe (recall, decide)*. . . . In the former case the obstacles the person had to overcome must have affected his speech (sluggish tongue, outside noise, etc.). In the latter case the obstacles must have been "inside" him (prejudice, sluggish memory, etc.). This point I owe to Mr. David Brusegard.

that produces the edifice. For, no doubt, thinking is an activity, a process, something that goes on, which we can pursue, and of which we are aware throughout our conscious life. Thinking is the stream of consciousness, the 'buzzing-blooming confusion' of images, sounds, feelings, and emotions; interspersed, it is true, by words or even sentences dimly 'heard,' subvocally 'pronounced,' or 'glanced at' with the mind's eye. To phrase my objection somewhat differently, you have confined your attention to *thinking that* . . . and to the objects of *thinking that* . . . , while ignoring *thinking about* . . . and *thinking of*. . . . And these ways of thinking are indeed processes according to your own criteria. We ask, in the progressive tense, 'What are you thinking about?' and we say 'I was thinking about you all the time. . . .' Moreover, the philosophically interesting sense of *thinking* is obviously this process sense: the process of thinking constitutes our 'inner life'; and this is the thinking of which we are really aware, the one that remains inaccessible to others. Thinking in the propositional sense, *thinking that* . . . , is rather like a disposition to say certain things and to behave in one way rather than another. For, surely, we are not aware, at any given time, of all that we think in the propositional sense. A man sound asleep may be said to 'think' (i.e., to believe, suspect, want, regret, etc.) many things in this sense, without doing any thinking at that moment."

I reply to the second half of the objection first. What the objector says is like claiming that speaking is really *talking about*, not *saying that*. Talking about something is indeed an activity one pursues, a process that goes on. As we ask "What is he thinking about?" we also ask "What is he talking about?" in the progressive tense. Talking about something is carried on in a process of talking, in producing a patterned sequence of noises. Yet, clearly, the mere utterance of sounds, in no matter what sequence, does not amount to talking about anything. Parrots and dolls may talk in this sense, yet they cannot talk *about* anything. For, as we remarked above, they cannot say anything in the full sense of the word. And no one can talk about anything without saying something in the process, that is, without performing some illocutionary acts. Thinking about (or thinking of) something also involves a process of "thinking." The images, the sounds, the subvocal words, what have you, all may be there, but, again, no such succession of images will constitute the process of thinking about (or of) something, unless these "images" carry some mental acts. Animals, probably, can "think" in the sense of having internal experiences of a similar kind; what they cannot do is to think about something. In talking about something a person performs a series of illocutionary acts: he may assert, suggest, or argue that something is the case; describe and rate a person or a thing; recommend, urge, or advise a certain course of action; and so on. In thinking about something one goes through a series of mental acts, often involving some changes of mental states: one may guess, assume, realize, or conclude that something is the case; regard, consider, or view a certain thing in many ways; contemplate, plan, and decide to do one thing or another; and wonder about consequences. One also might adopt beliefs, give up suspicions, modify intentions—that is, "make up" or "change one's mind" in these and many other ways. The idea that one might be thinking about something without performing any of these or similar acts is as incomprehensible as the idea of talking about something without saying anything at all.

These reflections enable us to answer the first point about the process-product confusion. Between thinking and building *nego paritatem*. Not because buildings are visible and thoughts are not, not even because the result of building, the edifice, is physically distinct from the agent, while the alleged result of thinking, the thought, is not; but simply because the process of thinking, thinking about or thinking of, involves and presupposes thoughts, whereas the process of building does not involve and presuppose edifices already in existence. Remember, once more, the analogy of speech: talking about something is to be understood in terms of saying something, not the other way around; saying something is not the product of talking about something. Similarly, having a thought is not the product of thinking about something; it is rather this latter notion that involves the former: thinking about something consists in conceiving and entertaining a series of thoughts. The builder may stop building without having completed any edifice; the thinker who stops thinking, on the other hand, already must have had some thoughts.

12. In the reply just given I relied heavily on the parallelism of speech and thought, on the analogy of proportionality between saying something and talking about something on the one hand, and thinking something and thinking about something on the other. I even let myself be lured into suggesting that, speaking somewhat poetically, as external noisemaking is the carrier of speech, internal image-making is the carrier of thought. Yet this cannot be. For whereas speech is the expression of thought in a code—that is, by means of a language— thought is not an expression of anything and is not conceived in a code or *via* a code.

It may happen that through the ignorance of a particular language I fail to understand what someone else has said, or even what I myself recite in that tongue. It may also happen that a sentence in my native tongue, heard, read, or uttered by myself, escapes my understanding. It is inconceivable, however, that I might fail to understand what I think. Hearing the speaker's voice, or seeing his writing, is indispensable for getting at what he said, but what do I have to see or hear, externally or in my mind, to get at my own thoughts? I do not deny that some inner experiences may accompany our thinking about something: the confusion of images, sounds, or even of words, phrases, and sentences, mentally heard, seen, or vocalized, in this language or in that, may be there, but their possible presence has nothing in common with the necessity of using a language in talking about something. Such accompaniments of thinking are by no means all internal: postures (like that of Rodin's "Thinker"), frowns ("thoughtful" frowns), mumblings ("thinking aloud"), gestures, and so forth, may go with thinking as well, in much the same way as smiles and grimaces, gestures and posturings, may accompany our speech without affecting what we say. But, in the case of speech, such trappings are to be distinguished from the code-elements, that is, the words, structures, intonation patterns, and the like that convey the message. These, but not the smiles and the sighs, *belong* to the language, are the elements of a highly complex and learned code. With thought, all the things we mentioned, external and internal, are mere accessories; there is no message to encode and no private language to use for the encoding.

If you say something to me, you must know what you want to say. Otherwise, even if your mouth pronounces words, you would merely parrot something but not say anything. I, on the other hand, have nothing but your words to go on; these are the medium through which I have to get the message. Naturally, I might not get it. You may have chosen inappropriate words, I may not know the language well enough, you may have committed a slip of the tongue, or I may have misheard you. Thus it is always possible that I fail to understand you or that

Res Cogitans

I misunderstand you. And this possibility is inherent in any use of any code: encoding and decoding can be correct or incorrect. Now if thinking needed a code, consisting of words or other symbols; if, in other words, thinking were something like talking to oneself silently; then, on the one hand, the thinker would know what he wanted to "say" to himself, but on the other, he could be mistaken about what he did "say." In other words, it would be possible for him to know and not to know what he thinks at the same time.

This is absurd, of course, but the absurdity crops up earlier still. Concerning speech, which involves encoding—that is, putting thoughts into words—it makes sense to speak of what somebody wanted to say but could not, because, for example, he did not know the language or was affected by aphasia. What would it be, on the other hand, to want to think something yet being unable to do so because of some malfunctioning of the mental "medium" or because of one's deficient command over the same?

13. If thinking is not identical with the flux of words and images we perceive in the imagination, then—the question arises—how are we aware of our own thoughts? Or, shall we agree with our objector and admit that our thoughts—our beliefs, suspicions, decisions, intentions, regrets, and so on—are merely dispositions?

In the first place I can see some, but not much, plausibility to the view that beliefs, suspicions, and other mental states are dispositions. A mental state normally has an effect on what people do and say. By observing them and listening to their words we might gather some clues as to what they know, believe, or intend to do, even if they do not explicitly reveal in words what these things are, much as we can gather the condition of muscles, bones, and nerves from the way people walk, limp, or hobble. Of course, in either case, the subject of our observation might choose not to reveal anything or mislead us on purpose: the witness can stand mute or prevaricate, and the patient can lie prone or dance and grin and bear it. If people's knowledge, beliefs, and intentions consisted in some pattern of their overt behavior, the task of poker players, spies, diplomats, detectives, interrogators, and inquisitors would be easy indeed, and thumbscrews and racks would never have been heard of. As a broken bone does not consist in limping and the like, one's intention to go to Paris does not consist in poring over the map of France, or doing similar things.

In order to assess the dispositional account of mental states, it is illuminating to compare such states with certain human traits that are indeed but dispositions. If we say that a person is generous or mean, patient or irritable, polite or uncouth, we ascribe to him a fairly permanent, and fairly predictable, pattern which marks some relevant domains of his behavior, normally without implying anything about his mental states. After all, a person may be irritable or uncouth without wanting to be, or even without knowing that he is. Thus with respect to these characteristics, it is possible for us to know that a certain person has them, without himself being aware of the fact. Thus there would be no point in "putting him to the question" (on the rack or otherwise) to induce him to reveal what he knows but we do not. All we have to do is to observe him with care. For if a person's urbanity, patience, or generosity never manifests itself, then, whatever he may think of himself, the person is not polite, patient, or generous.

This is obviously not so with mental states. Take, for instance, an expert of Roman history; think of all the information, all the beliefs, assumptions, guesses and suspicions he might have concerning his subject. Then ask yourself whether it is necessary, or even possible, for him to display all these mental states, in word or deed, in order to have them. Again, some people's consciences are burdened with guilty secrets from their past, which they would not reveal in any circumstances. And, speaking of guilty secrets, what about the professional secrecy incumbent upon priests, lawyers and doctors concerning the revelations of their clients? The father confessor must not reveal, either by word or by deed, in any circumstances whatsoever, what he has been told *sub sigillo*. Does the requirement of unconditional secrecy demand something inconceivable? Yet the confessor knows these secrets, and normally believes what he has been told.

"Still, he *could* tell you what he knows, as the historian too could voice or otherwise manifest his beliefs, *if* he wanted to." This is the last line of defence for the dispositional account, that so-called mental states are not so much a matter of actual, but rather of hypothetical behavior—what the agent would do and say if. . . . This is like an appeal to sleeping witnesses: what they would have seen had they been awake. Let us consider once more real dispositions. Take Joe, who does not display any courtesy toward his fellow men; he is certainly not polite in anybody's book. Now could one save his reputation by arguing that he would behave otherwise if he wanted to, or if he were placed in circumstances that in fact never occurred? Obviously not, since all this amounts to is that Joe could be polite if he wanted to, or would be polite given such and such. It does not follow at all, however, that he *is* polite now. Therefore, if mental states were indeed bona fide dispositions, then by merely suggesting what people would do or say in certain possible circumstances one would only account for what they would believe, suspect, or whatever *in those circumstances*, and not for what they do believe or suspect now. The logic of dispositional terms indeed involves the conditional. The assertion that somebody is polite is not a mere description; it warrants projections too: "Since Jim is polite, he will (or would) yield his scat." But in sayng that he is polite we also imply some actual facts. It comes down to this: it makes perfect sense to say that Sherlock Holmes suspected the butler all along, but gave no sign of it; it is nonsense to say, however, that he was polite to the butler all along without showing any sign of it.

It does not help to insist that a dispositional predicate may be true of a subject without any actual manifestation—for example, that a vase may be brittle without ever actually breaking. Granted, but in that case one must have some other ground for saying that it is brittle—for example, that it is made of glass (i.e., has a certain molecular structure). But if, say, Holmes never met the butler, what other reason could there be for claiming that nevertheless he was polite to the man? We have to realize, therefore, that whereas politeness is a "pure" disposition, brittleness is not. In either case the unfulfilled hypotheticals are but a projection from a categorical base. In the case of pure dispositions (politeness, generosity, and the like), that base must be actual behavior (the man *did* behave politely on a number of occasions); in the case of, let us say, "mixed" dispositions (brittleness, elasticity, and the like), it may be *either* actual behavior *or* some actual state (e.g., internal structure).

Hence it is clear that mental states cannot be pure dispositions. Holmes suspected the butler from the beginning without showing any sign of it. For this reason we did not know whom he suspected, but he certainly did know. On the other hand, if he did not show any politeness toward the butler, we cannot say that although we did not know that he was polite toward the butler, he did. His suspicion, therefore, must comprise an actual state, which can subsist and can be known independently of any manifestations.

What then are these mental states? One might wish to cast a final doubt upon their independent existence by pointing out that whereas molecular structures, broken bones, and torn ligaments can be directly observed by means of the electron microscope, the X-ray machine, or the naked eye, beliefs, intentions, and the like cannot. True, but this merely shows that mental states are not observable entities. If I am asked whether I believe that Paris is a beautiful city, or whether I intend to go there next summer, I do not have to observe or recall my conduct to answer truthfully. I do not have to "observe" my beliefs and intentions either; I merely voice them or express them in words. It may happen that I do not know how to answer such questions. Do I think that Madrid is a lively place? If I have no set opinion on this particular matter, I may try to form one, try to "make up my mind" about it. This may take some thinking based on certain facts I can recall about Madrid—and not about my actual or possible behavior.

Notice how different it is with real dispositions. There the subject and the observer are in the same boat. To find out whether you are polite, patient, or generous, you and I have to rely on the same evidence: your conduct in the relevant circumstances. Therefore you too can be mistaken in these matters, and be corrected by other people. As for your mental states, I need evidence (your words and actions); you do not. It would be rather odd to suggest that you yourself should recall your past actions to find out what you believe, whom you suspect, and what you intend to do, and it would be ludicrous to add that you should ask me, or other observers, about it.

If you ask a man whether he is polite, he may answer falsely for two reasons: he may be mistaken, or he may be lying. If, on the other hand, you ask him whether he believes that he is polite, his answer can be false only if he is lying. Thus whereas a man may honestly claim that he is polite, and be in fact impolite, nobody can honestly claim that he believes that he is polite, while in fact not believing that he is. With real dispositions the subject's own claim stands on a par with the verdicts of other observers, that is, it can be challenged for honesty or truth. With mental states his words enjoy a "privileged" status: to challenge them is tantamount to assailing his honesty, since the escape hatch of possible error is barred.

Or consider: if a friend of mine is accused of a crime, I may try to believe that he is innocent, or—if I do not succeed— I may at least try to behave as if I believed that he is innocent. Now if belief were a disposition, these two endeavors would amount to the same thing. And they do not.

With respect to mental acts the dispositional account loses even the initial plausibility. Decisions are often sudden, and recognitions and realizations normally take but a moment. I just decided not to go to the movies tonight. This may be true, no matter what I do afterward, even if I call up the theater for reservations. For I could have changed my mind or decided to fool you. I may be the only one who will ever know what I have decided in my heart.

One final point. I have granted above that mental states often indeed dispose a person to act in one way or another; they are apt to mold one's acts. But, again, these acts themselves may be mental acts; mental states may mold one's mental "behavior." If Joe loves Mary, he will not merely try to please her and seek her company, he will also often think about how to please her and how to find her company. Love, of course, is a "mixed" state, part of it being emotion. But the same is true of purely mental states. Take intentions: my intention to go to France will govern, in part, my thoughts at least as much as my overt acts. Moreover, the implications may be mental altogether. One may resolve not to think about something or other (say a threat, an unworthy suspicion, or the like). As a result, the person will avert or cut off such thoughts when they emerge. So, I ask, what is the point of trying to explain mental states in terms of overt behavior if mental acts, at least, have to be admitted anyway?

14. How do I know my own mental acts? How do I know what I just decided; how do I know what I believe, what I suspect, what I intend to do? These are one and all silly questions. But the fact that they are silly is instructive. It indicates that we are aware of these mental acts and states immediately, not less than of the sensations we feel, the pains we suffer, and the mental images we entertain. As it is silly to ask somebody, "How do you know that you are in pain?" it is equally foolish to ask, "How do you know that you want to go to the movies?" [2] We do not conclude to the existence of our beliefs or intentions on the basis of observing our own actions any more than we discover the existence of our headache by looking into a mirror. Nor, for that matter, do we have to listen to our own voices to know what we are saying, or watch our limbs to find out what we are doing, except in some abnormal situations.

This common feature of "immediate awareness" may be behind the temptation to confuse thought with sensations, feelings, mental images, and the like. Yet these things, the "buzzing blooming confusion" of consciousness, have very little to do with thought. Much thinking may cause headache, but the headache does not add to the thinking; it is likely to stop it.

[2] In Chapter VII, I am going to show that sensations and feelings are, in fact, much less "immediate" than our thoughts.

Thoughts

So are other strong sensations, emotions, compulsive images, feelings of pain, dizziness, nausea, and so forth. These are not thinking, nor do their tamer cousins amount to thinking when they occur in dreams, daydreams, reveries, or mindless contemplations. The process of thinking may be accompanied, however, by all sorts of mental images, as we have conceded above, but this remains accidental. What I say essentially depends upon the words I pronounce; what I think is essentially independent of the play of my imagination. This latter may help or distract; St. Antony in the desert has been disturbed by the lascivious play of his imagination while meditating upon the holy mysteries, yet he carried on bravely; the mathematician and the chess player, on the other hand, are likely to evoke certain images to aid their thinking. It stands to reason, too, that words, or even sentences, are apt to crop up in the imagination, while thinking about something. After all, these are the normal means of expressing the thoughts the thinker entertains; no wonder they are closely linked together. Often such words break into the open: the thinker begins to mumble or even gesticulate.

Yet if, say, a mathematician thinks about a problem, that is what he thinks about no matter what goes on in the background of his fancy. He may see shapes or flashes of lights; he may hear music or human voices. Some of these may help, others hinder; but all are compatible with his thinking about that problem, and so is the absence of any imagery. He is not bound to use any images in his thinking, as he is bound to use certain words in telling us what he found out. Speech needs a language; thought does not.

IV

Propositions

1. The results of the previous chapter give the impression of a paradox. On the one hand, we have concluded that thoughts are not framed in words, yet, on the other, we have insisted on the identity of what can be thought and what can be said. Somebody might argue, therefore, that since whatever we say must be constructed out of words, one of these two claims must be mistaken.

I reply by denying the opponent's premise, namely, that what we say is something constructed out of words. What we say, in the full sense of this word, is a thought expressed in words, couched in words; whereas the same thought, unexpressed and not coded in words, may be the object of a mental state or a mental act, say, of a belief or a realization. Consequently, throughout the following discussion, I could use the word *thought* to denote this common object, and, as I have pointed out in the previous chapter, such a usage would not be inconsistent with our normal way of talking about these matters.[1]

[1] See Chapter III, section 9.

Propositions

In order to avoid a possible ambiguity, however, I shall use a familiar technical term, *proposition,* to refer to this common object, and I shall reserve the name *thought* for such an entity insofar as it is the object of a mental act or state only, that is, insofar as it remains unexpressed in words. Finally, I shall use the word *message* to denote propositions expressed in words.

2. Toward the end of Chapter II we distinguished two senses of the word *say,* the "full" sense and the "weak" sense. To say something in the full sense is to perform an illocutionary act—to make a statement, give a promise, issue an order, or what have you. The weaker sense of *say,* on the other hand, involves the mere utterance of a word, or words, or at least of something articulate, something that "sounds" like a word, or words, belonging to a human language. For saying, even in this sense, is not just making some vocal noises: coughing, hissing, crying, and howling are not forms of saying, nor do dogs and cats say anything when they bark or purr. Parrots, on the other hand, can be taught to say words or even sentences. Similarly, humans can say things in the weaker sense only when, for instance, they utter words to practice their pronunciation, when they repeat sentences or lists to memorize them, when they recite tongue-twisters, rigmaroles and the like. On can "say" nonsense syllables too: they are like words in that they consist of phonemes, whereas coughs and sneezes, barks and purrs, do not.

These two ways of saying things are reflected in the two characteristic ways of reproducing what one said, which are commonly known as direct and indirect quotation. Things said in the weak sense cannot be reproduced indirectly. This is immediately obvious with respect to nonsense syllables, individual words, or groups of words such as lists, that do not coalesce into a sentence: the child said "bim-bam-boom" or "ante, apud, ad, adversus." What he said would not fit into the *that*-clause of the indirect quotation. In case a full sentence has been uttered the clause is normally available but its use is restricted to the instances of saying something in the full sense, that is, to the performances of illocutionary acts.

Suppose I teach an average four-year-old child to say "Thou art a craven knave." After some effort he may say "Thou art a craven knave." It would be wrong, however, for me to report: "He just said that I was a craven knave" or "He just called me a craven knave." I cannot say the former because I cannot say the latter: the child's performance did not amount to the illocutionary act of calling somebody something, nor to any other illocutionary act; consequently the word *say* in the full sense, and by the same token the indirect quotation, is out of place in this case. Remember that *say*, in this sense, is a general performative.

How do I know that the child did not perform an illocutionary act? This question, of course, leads to another one: if I assume that a speaker did perform an illocutionary act, what does this assumption entail? At the end of Chapter II I gave a hint: to put it roughly, the speaker must have understood what he was saying and he must have meant it.

The trouble with the child is that I have no reason to think that he understood what he said. But what about me, who uttered that sentence many times over while teaching him? Did I call that poor child, repeatedly, a cowardly rogue? Obviously not. Yet I certainly understood what I was saying; at least in the sense of understanding the sentence I uttered. The trouble with my performance, of course, is that I did not intend to call the poor mite that awful name. The moral of the story is simple on the surface: the proposition that X said that *p* entails, first, that X understood the sentence he uttered and, second, that he intended to perform the appropriate illocutionary act.

Propositions

These are necessary conditions but even jointly not sufficient. Austin's doctrine of "infelicities" reminds us that speech-acts may misfire for reasons other than lack of understanding or due intention. But this is another, and a better known story. What we want to tell is the story of understanding and intention. And this requires some spadework.

3. In giving a direct quotation the speaker has to repeat the utterance in question word by word intact. Indirect quotations, on the other hand, rarely reproduce the utterance without some change, and—as we are going to see—ideally, they never do. The difference is not merely a matter of *that* versus quotation marks; this is but the tip of the iceberg.

What is the general form of an indirect quotation? Oddly enough, I do not know of any study taking up this matter in a systematic way. Philosophers in this century have spent much more time in trying to get rid of indirect discourse than in trying to understand what they want to get rid of.

Yet, in the light of Austin's investigations, this much is clear to begin with: indirect quotation is not a repetition of a sentence somebody uttered, but a report on a speech-act somebody performed. As saying something consists in the performance of an illocutionary act, telling what somebody said will consist in specifying the illocutionary act that person performed. Consequently any such report will begin by indicating the illocutionary force: He *stated . . . suggested . . . promised . . . ordered . . . praised . . .* etc. The neutral *say* (or even *tell*) may, as we know by now, stand in for nearly all of these specific performatives.[2]

We also know that in many cases the actual use of the performative is omitted in the original speech-act if the circum-

2 See Chapter II, section 14.

stances, as it were, speak for themselves; for example, the commanding officer rarely has to prefix *I order* to his orders. Whether the performative is there or not, however, in reporting the order I have to use the verb *order* or the neutral substitute *say* (or *tell*): *He ordered . . .* or *He said . . .* (*He told . . .*).

This raises an intriguing possibility. Suppose my commanding officer orders me to attack, and to make sure I get it right, he uses the explicit performative: he says "I order you to attack." I, however, settle for *say* in my report. How will it run? Certainly not *He said that he ordered me to attack.* This would be both ungrammatical and misleading. *He said that he had ordered me to attack:* this is grammatically all right but clearly false. *He said that I should attack:* this is correct and true, but vague: *say*, the general performative, replaces the specific verb *order*, which move leaves the illocutionary force unspecified. The only construction that lets in both words is (at least to this speaker): *He said that he orders me to attack.* This is an interesting specimen. The tense goes from *order* to *say*, leaving *order* tenseless—a bloodless appendage to *say*.

These reflections show that indirect quotation does not by any means consist in a blind application of *said that* followed by the original utterance or some slightly revised version of it. Nor is the particle *that* necessary, or even desirable in many instances: *He ordered me to . . .* , *He promised to . . .* , *He called me . . .* , *He apologized for . . .* , and so forth. In general, the structure of the reproduction is as much a function of the particular performative as the structure of the original product.

Finally, considering that the normal, or rather ideal, form of an utterance endowed with an illocutionary force always contains the present perfect of the performative with the particle

I before it, it is quite clear that no such utterance can be reproduced indirectly without at least one change: the addition of the past-tense mark.[3] Moreover, whenever we reproduce what someone else has said we have to change the first person pronoun into something else. The *I*, of course, and a present performative will be there again, but in a different place. For the whole report is my report, and it is a report (or statement, testimony, etc.). So the normal form of indirect quotation will begin with *I report* . . . or some variant. This completes the general form of such quotations, which is this:

$$I \, V_p \, \text{nom}(N_h \, t(V_p) \, \text{nom}(N \, V+))$$

where the suffixes mean *performative* (verb) and *human* (noun) and *t* indicates the tense-mark (past) on the second performative. *Mutatis mutandis* the same schema works for other forms of indirect discourse, that is, for the reproduction of someone else's, or my own, thoughts as well.

4. It appears, then, that what indirect quotation shares with what it reproduces is represented by *nom* $(N \, V \, +)$ in our formula. Grammatically this is nothing but the familiar noun-clause, which makes up the verb-object of all propositional verbs. Somebody might suggest, therefore, that what is being said in a speech-act, and what is being reproduced in an indirect quotation, is nothing but a noun-clause. Since in view of what we have found thus far in this chapter the nominalistic dream of regarding sentences as the things said is clearly untenable, the nominalist might embrace this new possibility: if not sentences, why not noun-clauses? They, like sentences, are made up of words, so there is no need to go beyond flesh and blood, or

[3] Except the dubious exception of *He said that he orders* . . . and the like.

57

rather larynx and air (or paper and ink), reality in our search for the mystery of what is said.

Unfortunately, even this substitute dream is destined to a rude awakening as we recall that *say* in this context is but a colorless understudy to a cast of colorful performatives. Consequently, if our nominalist wants to maintain that what we say are noun-clauses, he must also be willing to swallow the nonsense that it is noun-clauses which we state and suggest, order and promise, that it is they we object to and apologize for. Needless to say, no harmless grammatical construction, such as the noun-clause, is the worthy object of such concerns.

Rhetorics aside, it is easy to show that no sentence, no noun-clause, in fact no string of words whatever, can be what one says. I shall advance four arguments for this conclusion.

The first one is taken from the use of personal, possessive, and demonstrative pronouns, names, and other devices of reference. If Joe, the suspect of petty larceny, says at the police station "I stole the watch," then, if the circumstances are all right, the police may justly claim that Joe admitted that he had stolen the watch. Now if what Joe said had been the sentence *I stole* . . . or the noun-clause *that I stole* . . . , then the police would have no right to claim that what he said was that *he* had stolen the watch. Similar word-switches will be necessary to reproduce what Joe said about his wife, his debts, the watch in front of him, and so forth. At this point it does not help to bring in the matter of referential opacity.[4] Quine's point is extremely important, and it will be taken up later on. For our present purposes, however, it is sufficient to realize that the opaqueness of indirect discourse depends upon the original speaker's supposed ignorance of certain referential equivalences: the trouble arises because he does not know (or might not know), for in-

[4] See W. V. Quine, *From a Logical Point of View*, Ch. VIII.

stance, what is the capital of Honduras, or the other name of Cicero. In the cases I am discussing, however, it would be absurd to suggest that the speaker (who, mind you, is supposed to know how to talk) might not know how to use *I* and *you*, *this* and *that*, *mine* and *thine* (or at least *yours*). He, in fact, will expect me to make the appropriate switches and would protest if I did not. Yet, clearly, the word *I* is not the same as the word *he*, and the clause *that I stole* . . . is different from the clause *that he stole*. . . .

The police, therefore, are correct in claiming that what Joe admitted was that he had stolen the watch. The noun-clause closing the previous sentence, *that he had stolen the watch*, differs from Joe's original in another respect too; in the tense required by the *consecutio temporum*. Joe, who knows the language, cannot protest against this further distortion of his "sentence" either. Nor could he possibly object against the use of such "paraphrastic transforms" as the ones in *He admitted having stolen the watch*, . . . *that it was stolen by him*, . . . *that it was he who stole it*, and so on. Once more, he is (presumably) a fluent speaker of the language; consequently he must recognize that as he could have made the same admission by using any of these transforms, the police have every right to do the same in their account of what he said. For the same reason, had the policeman originally asked Joe the question "Did you steal the watch?" and had he answered "Yep," the police still would be fully entitled to claim that he admitted the theft of the watch. These observations on grammatical freedom constitute my second argument.

The phrase I just used, *the theft of the watch*, leads us to the third. The linguistic freedom we enjoy in indirect discourse extends beyond the domain of syntax. Indeed, in view of the virtual inseparability of syntax and semantics, it would be rather surprising if it did not. *Theft* can replace *stealing* in many contexts, and Joe's case is one of them. I have no fear of getting embroiled in the murky waters of the general problem of synonymy by simply pointing out the obvious truth that there are many individual circumstances in which it makes no difference, as to what one said, which of two words has been used. Often for reasons of good style or decency the indirect quotation is bound to make lexical changes without any loss of accuracy, albeit with some loss of the original "flavor." Even if Joe had enlightened the court concerning the disposal of his ill-gotten gain by the words "I blew the dough," it would be perfectly correct for the judge to say in his summation that Joe admitted that he had spent the money recklessly. The reason for this particular freedom is analogous to the one mentioned before: the original speaker as well as the other participants of the discourse are supposed to know the language they use, so that they must be credited with the ability not only to see through the opaqueness of elementary referential situations, but also to recognize simple paraphrases, be they the result of mere syntactical reshuffle or of some replacement in the dictionary entries used. For if Joe, for instance, does not know the language, how can he say anything in it, when saying something presupposes the understanding of the sentence used? In our example, therefore, Joe cannot possibly object even if the morphology of the sentence he used gets progressively distorted beyond recognition in the course of indirect reproduction, provided that he, as the speaker of the language, still recognizes it as a correct expression of what he said.

There are, of course, limits to any speaker's command of the language. If we tell Joe that he just confessed to having abstracted the timepiece, he might protest that he did not say anything like that.[5] If he does not know these words, he will neither know how to paraphrase them nor what they can be used to paraphrase. By the same token, if he were to object to all paraphrases of his original sentence, we would be entitled to conclude that he did not understand what he was saying and consequently that he did not admit anything, did not *say* anything in the full sense of the word.

The fourth argument involves the really difficult matter of translation. Since I have not discussed the problem of inter-translatability between languages, and do not wish to do so at this point, I will give the argument in a very brief form. People exposed to the diversity of languages are conscious of the possibility of discussing in their native tongue views expressed by speakers of other languages, of agreeing and disagreeing with them, and so forth, and they are willing to grant the reciprocal right to those foreigners. Now, surely, if I can say in English what Descartes said in Latin, or if I can contradict in English what Descartes said in French, then what Descartes said, and what I say, cannot be a string of words, English, Latin, or French.

5. We have seen that the possibility of indirect reproduction is conceptually tied to the performance of an illocutionary act. And we have demonstrated in detail that indirect reproduction does not and cannot consist in a mere repetition of the speaker's words. It follows, therefore, that to perform an illocutionary act is to license the reproduction of what one says in a way in which the fidelity to words is superseded by a concern to preserve something else. This is by no means true, of course, of the "weak"

[5] Joe would be wrong, of course; yet, in view of his linguistic deficiency, he would have some reason to demur.

cases of saying: there the words are essential; any replacement or reshuffle would spoil the appropriate reproduction. In saying something in the "full" sense, however, the speaker intends his words to be mere instruments, which can be replaced by equivalent ones, and should be replaced if, say, the exigencies of reference, grammar, and style demand some changes. To give a new twist to an older terminology, in saying something in the full sense, words are "used" in accordance with their natural use, that is, as instruments employed in the performance of an illocutionary act. The word *use* is very appropriate here: one uses tools to do a job, and the same job may be done by using other tools; tools are replaceable. Yet words are tools of a specific kind: we do not ask someone to "say it *with* other words," but rather to "say it *in* other words." This is similar to "Say it *in* German" or "Put it *in* writing." We convey a message *in* a code and not *with* a code. The underlying metaphor is clear enough: words are like vessels that carry a content. In the weak cases of saying the words are pronounced, "mentioned" if you like, but not used according to their proper use. The instructions "Say some other words" and "Say some German words" can be obeyed without saying something in words or in German.

The exact nature of the speaker's intention determines the particular illocutionary force of his utterance. If, for instance, in saying "I'll be there" my intention is to cause you to believe or to expect, by means of your recognition of my intention from these words, that I shall be there, then what I say is intended to have the force of a statement or a forecast. If, however, my intention in saying those words is to entitle you to rely on my going there, then it will have the force of a promise. If, finally, those words are intended to make you fear my going there (say, in order to deter you from doing something against me), then it will be a threat. Accordingly, if the circumstances are not clear, I will attach a sign, usually a performative verb (or an intonation pattern for the threat) to explicitly mark the force. And you, of course, if you fully understand what I say, will know, first, that it is my going there that I, by using these words, intend you to come to expect, rely upon, or fear, and, second, which one of these "illocutionary aims" I wanted to achieve. Whether you, in fact, will come to expect, rely upon, or fear my going there or not is as irrelevant to the uptake of the message as the overt action, if any, you might perform as a result of my statement, promise, or threat.[6]

We have to distinguish, therefore, both in the speaker's intention and in the hearer's understanding, the message itself—in our case, that I shall be there—and the illocutionary force with which this message is issued. Moreover, the same content, the same proposition—that I shall be there—may (if I am honest) or may not (if I am not) be the object of my belief, and may become yours if you believe me. Obviously, the same distinction between the message and the force is mirrored in the distinction between the devices of the language that serve to encode the content, and the devices that serve to mark the illocutionary force. To say something, therefore, is to issue a message encoded in a language and marked (explicitly or implicitly) by a performative.

6. Let us return to our four-year-old friend and the sentence *Thou art a craven knave.* We both, the child and I, uttered this sentence. He did not even understand it; I did, but did not mean to say anything by uttering it. Concerning the first notion

---

[6] These last remarks are largely inspired by H. P. Grice's paper "Meaning" (*The Philosophical Review*, LXVI [July 1957], 377–388). Incidentally, the emphatic phrase . . . *and I mean it!* is used to stress the illocutionary force of the utterance, which fact reinforces our contention that to mean what one says is to endow one's utterance with an illocutionary force.

it seems to be clear, in the light of what we just said, that understanding a sentence has to be explained in terms of knowing what "message" that particular sentence can carry. Unfortunately, this rather vague idea will not account for the human ability to understand a potentially infinite set of sentences; invoking a potentially infinite set of messages offers no solution. A finite set of elements, together with a recursive procedure, is what is needed here, and one will be outlined in Chapter VI.

Concerning the second notion, we begin to see the light. In pronouncing those words I did not intend to induce any belief in that child, or in anybody else; nor did I intend to achieve any other illocutionary aim. I merely mentioned those words, but did not use them according to their natural purpose; consequently I did not license any indirect reproduction: what I said was mere words, those exact words, vessels without content.

Spectators, if any, might have gathered this much from the circumstances. Yet circumstances do not constitute intentions. If, in a game, one player kicks another, a sharp-eyed spectator might be able to tell whether it was done intentionally—but again he might not. In certain circumstances only the kicker knows for sure. Of course, a kick is a kick, intentional or not; saying something, on the other hand, must be intentional. In this respect it is more like murder than like kicking. An unintentional "murder" is no murder. This similarity is not surprising. After all, saying something is doing something—and an *actus humanus* at that, like murder, not merely an *actus hominis*, like an unintentional kick.

7. At this point I expect an objection along the following lines. "Your distinction between the mysterious 'message' and the words that carry it reminds one of the old conception of money: there are the bank notes and the coins, but these things have

value only because they represent the nation's gold reserve deposited in the vaults of Fort Knox or some such place. So if I give you $5.00, it does not matter whether I give you a five-dollar note, five one-dollar notes, five hundred pennies, or any other equivalent combination out of the available notes and coins, since what I really give you is a chunk of gold represented by these tokens. But, you see, there is very little gold left in Fort Knox, and even if there were not any, we still could have our currency, and the interchangeability of tokens, which is similar to the interchangeability of words you harp on. Money can have its value even if there is no gold to back it up, and words can have their meaning even without the 'message' you imagine behind them. Consequently, if I report that, say, John gave Mary $5.00, this merely means that he either gave her a five-dollar bill, or he gave her five one-dollar bills, or—et cetera. Similarly, if you claim that John said such and such, it means that he uttered one member of a paraphrastic set of sentences. And, I grant you this, he must have done it with the intention of saying something. For words, and money, can be used unnaturally: one can use a penny as a screwdriver, and say 'cheese' to please the photographer. Remember, Russell has said that a proposition, which, I gather, is the equivalent of your 'message', is nothing but a paraphrastic set of sentences.[7] So I conclude with a more recent authority: the medium is the message. . . ."

Is it? If the conclusions drawn in the previous chapter are correct, then it is not. For we have seen, first, that what can be said can be thought, and, second, that thoughts are not couched in words, not even in alternative sets of words. The difficulties we encountered with the idea of thinking in words or images apply to any and all members of a paraphrastic set of sentences or phrases.

[7] E.g., in *An Inquiry into Meaning and Truth*, p. 10.

Moreover, at this point we can reinforce these arguments by mentioning some other differences between thinking and saying. If I tell you, in an indirect quotation, what Joe said on the witness stand, you still might want to know what his actual words were; for Joe must have used some in saying what he said. If, on the other hand, I tell you that I suspect Joe of having stolen the watch, it would be foolish for you to ask what the actual words of my suspicion are: do I suspect that he (or *Joe?*) stole the watch (or *swiped it?*), or that it was stolen by him, or, rather, do I suspect him of having stolen the watch, or what? My opponent will probably reply that since suspicion, like belief, is a disposition, it precisely consists (among other things) in a tendency to accept, or to produce, any of these variants. I do not agree, but let it pass. I ask, however, what about my coming to suspect or—given convincing evidence—coming to realize that Joe must have done it. These acts are not dispositions for sure, since they occur at a certain time but do not last. Yet even here the question about the exact words is misplaced. Suppose I tell you that last night I suddenly realized that Joe must have done it. Does it make sense to ask for the exact sentence I mentally pronounced (heard? read off?) in performing this act? Then take the case of my deciding not to prosecute. What am I supposed to have said to myself? "I shall not prosecute (or *press charges?*)" or "I decide not to prosecute"? The latter sentence may be deviant, and the former fails to show whether it was a decision or a mere forecast that I made.

The illocutionary aspect leads to another trouble. How can I say—even mentally—something to myself? If I say—really say—to you, "He must have done it," I claim your belief. But if my realization that he must have done it actually consists in my saying to myself, "He must have done it," then how can I claim my own belief in something which I already realize in making that very claim? Thus I cannot say something to myself in the full sense of *say*. Is it then enough if that sentence merely crosses my mind? This cannot be, since the wildest sentences may cross my mind without my realizing anything. "No" —my opponent argues—"you must *assent* to it; 'this is it,' you must feel." Thus I must *recognize* it as the one I need, must *realize* that it contains my realization—and the infinite regress is on its way.

Finally—and here I proceed on a well-beaten path—whereas such speech-acts as accusations and confessions take some time, depending on the length of the sentences in which they are expressed and the rapidity of one's speech, it just does not make sense to talk about long or short realizations and decisions— not to speak of the rapidity or slowness of their execution. A fast talker takes but a short time to *pronounce* what he has to say; a fast thinker takes but a short time to *arrive* at his conclusions, decisions, and the like. Again, it is possible to interrupt somebody's statement, accusation or apology in midsentence, but it is impossible to do the same to somebody's realization, decision, or regret. Speech-acts need sentences, mental acts do not.

Accordingly, I answer the objection by denying the parity between paper money and words. There is gold in this Fort Knox. What people state is often something they believe, what they promise is often something they have decided to do, and so on—and, even if not, it must normally be something they want the listener to come to believe, expect, et cetera. And these beliefs and expectations, decisions and intentions, are no more verbal, yet no less immediately obvious, than other mental acts and states.

8. I claimed above that to say something is to issue a message encoded in a language and that the same message can be issued

67

with a variety of illocutionary forces. Moreover, as I have amply demonstrated, the same proposition, which is the message expressed in a speech-act, can also be entertained, in the form of a thought, in a variety of mental acts and states.

Consider the following set of utterances:

I expect that you will occupy the city
I predict that you will occupy the city
I order you to occupy the city
I forbid you to occupy the city.

One is inclined to say that here the same proposition, your occupying the city, is claimed to be expected in thought and is being predicted, ordered, and forbidden in words. This is true, however, only under a big proviso, namely that the word *you* is used to refer to the same person and the phrase *the city* is used to denote the same city. This restriction raises the most serious difficulties for the views expressed in this chapter.

Hitherto, in dealing with nominalistic objections, we have relied upon the speaker's knowledge of the language to identify propositions in their linguistic garb. We have not yet explained how this task is achieved; it has been sufficient to realize that linguistic competence enables the speaker to employ, and the listener to see through, the variety of structural and lexical media available in a given language. We have even pointed out that the knowledge of one's language must include the mastery of such simple referential devices as the egocentric particulars, *I* and *you, this* and *that*, and so forth. Nobody can claim, however, that linguistic competence alone is sufficient to deal with the total referential situation in a given case. Clearly, to decide whether in the above examples *the city* does or does not denote the same city, the knowledge of the language is not enough. One has to know some facts, not about the language, but about the speakers, the circumstances, and geography. Consequently in order to understand what one said, it may not be sufficient to understand the sentence the speaker produced. To use Frege's terms: with respect to certain phrases the sense may be clear, and the reference not.

It appears, then, that at least some propositions combine sense and reference. Not all do, at least not in a way that would matter here. If you say, for instance, that love is a many-splendored thing, or that the square-root of 49 is 7, I can understand you without worrying about reference. Such "abstract" propositions, however, are the exception rather than the rule. As for the rest, the reference is distinct from the sense. Even if I understand the sentence *He loves that girl*, which you might use to say something, this does not guarantee that I will understand what you say when you do.

But suppose things turn out right, and I do. What does this mean? The answer seems to be simple: I have somehow succeeded in identifying him and her. From the context, from your gesture, or by following some added instructions (e.g., . . . *the girl in the red dress*) I "located" the boy and the girl. Shall we say, then, that such "concrete" propositions must contain some indexical element that points, as it were, to the referent? It seems so. For what else is the role of personal and demonstrative pronouns and of such "descriptions" as . . . *in the red dress* or . . . *over the hill* in the sentence expressing the proposition?

This view is plausible enough, yet it plays havoc with our conclusions previously established. We are faced with a dilemma and the possibility of having to retreat.

9. The dilemma shapes up as follows. We have seen above that in reporting what someone else has said, the second speaker

more often than not has to change the referential apparatus the first speaker has used (think of reproducing Joe's confession of the theft). Hence it seems to follow that the original referential device no more belongs to the proposition voiced by the first speaker than the other factors of syntax and vocabulary he used to code the message. As these are but replaceable garb, so is the particular way of referring; as the sense of the message can be abstracted from the carrier, so can the reference.

This position is untenable, however, in view of Quine's point about referential opacity. We have explained above that the reason for our liberty with the code-elements in reproducing what one said is the fact that the original speaker must be credited with the knowledge of the language he uses; and the knowledge of the language means, among other things, the ability to paraphrase and to recognize paraphrases. Alternative ways of referring, however, have nothing to do with paraphrasing; the speaker cannot be credited, automatically, with the knowledge of all referential equivalences. Consequently I have no unrestricted right to reproduce what he said by replacing the device of reference he used by one of my own choosing. Even if Joe said that Baghdad was in Iran, he did not say that the capital of Iraq was in Iran. He may be an ignoramus without being an imbecile. These facts seem to imply that the particular referential apparatus does belong to the proposition, to what one said. The dilemma is complete.

At our first encounter with the problem of referential opaqueness we suggested that its scope cannot include the use of such "pure" indicator particles as *I* and *you*, *this* and *that*. Indeed, it would be stultifying to suggest that my report that Joe admitted that *he* stole *that* watch might be incorrect or unfair because he used *I* and *this*. It must be granted, on the other hand, that in the Baghdad case the indicated way of reporting his statement would be both incorrect and unfair. What is the difference? Simply the following. In the Baghdad case there is a piece of relevant information that Joe does not have, namely that Baghdad is the capital of Iraq. But what information could he possibly lack in the other case? That I is he, or that this watch is that watch? These are pieces of nonsense and not of information.

Suppose I had reported Joe's assertion about Baghdad in the following fashion:

(1) Joe said that Baghdad, which is the capital of Iraq, is in Iran.

Is this correct or not? It depends. If I read it with the relative clause under the scope of *said* then not. Otherwise, yes. For, clearly, the clause *which is the capital of Iraq* is but a derivative of *Baghdad is the capital of Iraq*; *Baghdad* is replaced by *which* in view of the previous occurrence of the same noun. Joe, however, did not say that Baghdad was the capital of Iraq; I added it. Accordingly, *Joe said that . . .* cannot range over the clause. For the same reason any substitution based on the appositive clause will be illegitimate, will amount to smuggling in what I said, or what I know, into what Joe said. Of course he might have said this: "Baghdad, which is the capital of Iraq, is in Iran", in which case *said* in (1) indeed should include the clause, and I would be entitled to report that he said that the capital of Iraq was in Iran. Purely grammatically, (1) can be read in either way.

Next, consider the case in which Joe said, "Mary is a good cook." From the circumstances it is clear that the Mary in question is his wife. Can I report, then, that he boasted that his wife was a good cook? Undoubtedly, because I have every right to suppose that he knows his wife's name. If Mary, on the other hand, unbeknownst to poor Joe, is John's mistress, it would be wrong for me to report that Joe said (*boast* would not fit) that John's mistress was a good cook. But what if he knows of the sad state of affairs? Even then it would be at least odd to frame the report in those terms. The reason is that it is extremely unlikely that Joe would ordinarily think of his wife in those terms. Imagine Mrs. Nixon telling her daughter that the President is ill. What has been lumped together under the heading of referential opaqueness is a flock of more than one feather.

Compare these situations with Joe's consternation about his alleged admission of having abstracted the timepiece. He cannot or would not talk of his misdeed in these terms; hence the oddity of ascribing to him the admission thus phrased.

Where do all these observations leave us? On some middle ground between the horns of the dilemma. The referential factor cannot be entirely abstracted from the speaker's words and the speaker's mind. People speak about individuals in certain terms because they think about them in certain ways. They could not refer to something by using a description of which they do not know, and they would not do so by means of descriptions which are, even if known to them, unfamiliar, far-fetched, too complex, artificial, or otherwise remote. Propositions are subjective entities: statements, orders, promises, and so on are issued by persons; they are *their* statements, orders, and promises. In reproducing them I have to treat them as such, taking into consideration the speaker's mind: what he knows, how he thinks about this or that, or at least what he is likely to know, what are the ways he is likely to think about this or that. Thus it is not his actual words that really matter: those can be, and in many cases must be overridden; the restriction comes from the limitations of his mind, from the fact that an individual is known to a person only under some aspects—be they a series of spatiotemporal appearances or a set of descriptions. This point, the subjectivity of propositions, will assume great importance later on.

10. Propositions, we said, are the common objects of speech and of thought. If so, then the "taint" of subjectivity must affect not only statements, orders and promises, but also beliefs, suspicions, wants, decisions, intentions, and regrets. And it clearly does. For one thing, as it has been pointed out by Quine and others, referential opaqueness affects belief-contexts as much as it does indirect quotations. Hamlet wanted to avenge the murder of his father, not just of the previous king of Denmark; Oedipus regretted having married his mother, not just the lady named Jocasta. Moreover, as we just remarked, people are expected to talk about things in certain terms precisely because they can think about them only in certain terms.

With respect to thought, the idea of reference brings up an additional problem. In speech the most fundamental referring devices are indexical expressions, and then proper names. Descriptions, I believe, achieve reference to spatiotemporal individuals only insofar as they form a chain, actually given or presupposed in the discourse, leading to some "basic" individuals which have to be named or have to be pointed at in an ostensive situation.[8] It seems to me, moreover, that even the use of names is effective only because a similar chain connects them with things encountered in ostensive situations. If these assumptions are true, the worse for us; if they are not, matters are still bad enough. For, in either case, ostension and naming play an irreplaceable role in ordinary discourse. The problem is this: what in thought corresponds to ostension and naming? What, in

[8] At the end of my "Singular Terms" (in *Linguistics in Philosophy*), I discuss this matter in some detail.

73

other words, will discharge the same function in thought which the indexical particles (plus gestures, etc.) and names discharge in speech? Remember, we claimed that thought is not verbal and not image-bound, yet we want to maintain that (with some irrelevant exceptions) whatever one can say, one can think. I can say, for instance, that this book (in front of me) must be quite expensive, but John wants to buy it anyway. Can I not think the same thing? Can I not expect him to buy it without saying anything? And what about John's own desire to buy it (that book in front of him)? How are these things possible without words or images actually entering these very thoughts?

If descriptions could carry the ultimate burden of reference, if proper names and ostensive devices could indeed be dispensed with in every kind of discourse, as they can be in such "abstract" fields as mathematics or ethics, then we would not be in trouble. But they cannot, and we are. Descriptions, insofar as they do not contain names and indexicals, can be understood; names and indexicals, however, cannot. As the medievals said, there is no understanding of the individual; no concept can capture its *haecceitas*. We understand the "such," not the "this," and no amount of "such" congeals into a "this." The rationalists, *more geometrico cogitantes*, disdained images. We, thinking with the vulgar, might need some *phantasmata* after all.

We are forced to make a concession. But this is a retreat not a rout: our previous position needs to be adjusted, not abandoned.

What is it that reference achieves when successful? The listener "locates" the individual the speaker intended him to pick out. I said, "This book is valuable," while pointing at a book. John, the listener, guided by the gesture and the word *book* spots the book and understands that "it" is the one which

74

Propositions

I declared to be valuable. "It" to John means the book lying on its back on a table, thick, old, yellow, leatherbound, and so forth. What it is for something to be a book, to be old, to be bound in leather, to be lying on a table, and so on, are perfectly understandable ideas. What is not a matter for the understanding, however, is that these attributes are *de facto* realized, and realized in this one subject. For there is no logical nexus between them (at least not everywhere), and there is no logical nexus between any of them on the one side and existence on the other. That they *de facto* are realized at all, and realized in this subject, is a matter for the senses and not for the understanding.

If reference is to be successful the listener must do more than merely understand the referring phrase the speaker used. Suppose John is blind and paralyzed. He cannot see the book and cannot touch it either. Yet, if he is to understand what I said (and not merely the English sentence I used), he has to represent the situation around him in his imagination in such a way that the book appears in it as a visible, touchable *concretum*, an abode for an inexhaustible variety of attributes. This means that he must represent it in space and, in view of the changeability of at least some of the attributes, in time. And this space and time cannot be a mere abstract, mathematical system of dimensions, but something related to the momentary awareness of his body: he is supposed to imagine the situation around him starting from "here" and "now." He is the *origo* of this system of coordinates, which are designated in terms of "above" and "below," "left" and "right," "ahead" and "behind," "past" and "future," and which are measured in terms of "near" and "far."

Even in referring to individuals remote in space and time, the understanding of the reference will consist in establishing a spatiotemporal nexus to our present environment. The chain of descriptions connecting the two may be as simple as the one in *the city beyond that hill* or as complex and highly condensed as the one in *the emperor of Rome that died A.D. 180*. Things and events in the far recesses of space or at the early dawn of cosmic history can be spoken of and thought about insofar as they too belong to the spatiotemporal unity of the "manifold of experience." Otherwise, in Kant's words, they would be "nothing to us." True, one can refer to Zeus or to Hamlet, but this is by a special dispensation, parasitic upon the basic framework. For, after all, the former is supposed to have lived on Mount Olympus and the latter in Denmark. In fact they did not live anywhere, at any time; therefore in fact they are nothing.

The chain of descriptions along which we proceed toward the individual to be identified consists of intelligible elements: spatiotemporal relations and other connections that may hold between individuals. What is beyond the understanding and calls for the senses and the imagination is the fact that these spatiotemporal relationships obtain between concrete individuals and not between parts of empty space and time, and furthermore the fact that the cornerstone of the whole construction is the "here" and "now" of current experience. This reminds us of the medieval doctrine: the principle of individuation is *materia quantitate signata*. Matter, the subject of intelligible forms, in itself unintelligible, has to be pointed at (*signare*) in "quantity," that is, in extension and locus (the medieval equivalents of physical space). Putting it in a simple way: the purely indexical element of reference is not subject to the understanding. Experience and imagination must enter the very constitution of our thoughts involving concrete individuals.

Propositions

It may be argued that images cannot be part of the make-up of our mental states, since—given the multitude of our beliefs, suspicions, and intentions concerning individuals, with the imagination paying an intrinsic role in each—the result would be something resembling a film multiply exposed.

This is not so. For individuals in the spatiotemporal manifold cannot be represented as superimposed upon one another but as juxtaposed, together making up the unity of the manifold. To put it somewhat crudely: one picture is enough. And this "picture" is as immediately given to the thinking subject as the mental states themselves, for it is nothing but the empirical (i.e., self-centered) intuition of space and time. For, as Kant pointed out, this intuition is not empty and not finite; no single representation can be, as it were, cut off from the rest and viewed in empty space or time. Of course, not all beliefs, and not all elements of this "picture" are in the focus of one's attention at any given moment; sometimes none is (e.g., when one is sound asleep), sometimes a good portion is (think of the general making up his battle plan, taking into consideration a thousand and one facts, individuals, places, and times). Attended to or not, the beliefs are there, and so is the intuition of "here" and "now," placing the thinking subject in the world, and the world around the thinking subject.

The familiar analogy of the visual field may be helpful here.[9] If one's eyes are open, the whole of the visual field is seen, even if only some elements in it, or none at all (e.g., when one is absorbed in listening to music), are actually attended to. The thing we look at is "placed" with respect to the whole, and we ourselves are placed in a certain position by the very perspective of the visual field.

The question remains what "focusing one's attention" in

[9] See Wittgenstein, Tractatus, 5.63ff.

thought to any set of individuals might mean in this context. Since the question of attention is a moot one even in regard to actual experience, I do not feel particularly bad for not being able to give a very clear answer. From introspection it appears that it involves the exercise of the imagination to represent a "token" (image, voice, or just a name) which then stands for the individual in question. Even here the similarity between thought and speech holds good. Think of the various circumstances in which the phrase *that man* is used to achieve reference: the speaker may point at the person, his mirror image, his picture, his name on a list, his coat, the door of his office, and so forth. Similarly in thinking about, say, Rome, one's imagination may produce a skyline, a spot on a map, the name *Rome*, written or spoken, and the like. These variations do not matter. What matters in either case is that the token be accepted as standing for a particular individual that fits into the spatiotemporal manifold. One can imagine a lion very vividly without thinking of a particular lion at all. And one does not have to evoke even a vague image of a lion to think about a particular lion. A name might suffice, if it is taken as something belonging to *that* particular thing.[10]

11. Speaking of numbers, triangles, or moral virtues, the concept of reference applies only in an analogical sense. To be a triangle, to have three sides, and to have internal angles equal to 2R are necessarily connected (analytically or synthetically, but *a priori* at any rate). Consequently no empirical *concretum* is needed to hold these attributes together: questions of "where" and "when" are irrelevant. In thinking about these things the

[10] The arguments in this section often run parallel with Kant's reasoning in the "Analytic of Principles" (*Critique of Pure Reason*, B 169–315) and with P. F. Strawson's in *Individuals*, Part I, I.

role of the imagination is no less auxiliary than the actual use of an abacus or the drawing of diagrams on a blackboard. The diagram, or the mental image, has to be considered in an abstract fashion, by taking it out (*abstrahere*) of the empirical manifold centered around the "here" and the "now"; the images are viewed as objects of the understanding (or "pure" intuition, as Kant wants it); our attention is once more on the "such," not on the "this": I am thinking about the triangle (generic *the*), not about this triangle.

In this case, the abstraction in fact omits more than individuality: nothing beyond the necessarily connected attributes of spatial extension is relevant. We glance over such details as material, color, texture, and so forth. In Thomistic terminology, we make abstraction not only from individuality, but also from the sensory elements (*materia sensibilis*), retaining nothing but "intelligible" matter (*materia intelligibilis*).[11] The second move is not necessarily tied to the first. We just mentioned imagining a lion without taking it as a token for a particular lion. And, surely, a lion is not just a shape. Moreover, even the shape of a lion (whatever it is) is not something very intelligible to us. It is possible, therefore, to exercise the imagination in a sensory, yet abstract way. There is nothing surprising in this. Think of the pictures in a textbook of zoology: a picture may represent "a" lion, without representing any particular one. We are going to see in Chapter VI that with respect to certain empirical concepts this possibility acquires some importance.

Even for our present concern, we need sensory imagination in accounting for thoughts involving names, odd shapes, single words, and the like. One remembers the middle name of Cicero, one knows what the swastika stood for, and one might

[11] St. Thomas Aquinas, *In Boethium de Trinitate*, V. 3.

wonder what the word *Dummkopf* means. These mental acts and mental states would be impossible without the imagination producing, or at least being able to produce, some instances of the kinds involved. Here, indeed, I am willing to admit a dispositional account. If I know the middle name of Cicero, I am able to produce it in speech or writing, or imagine it as pronounced or written down.

12. The time has come to assess the extent of our retrenchment. It comes down to this: we are not God, and we are not angels either. We are not God, not only because we do not know everything, but also because even what we know we know only from a certain point of view, in terms of a limited set of descriptions. And we are not angels, because in thinking about individuals we have to represent them in a self-centered space and time, which procedure, of course, puts us into space and time ourselves.

Yet, though neither God nor angels, we need not be empiricists or behaviorists either. Our thinking about individuals may require a spatiotemporal framework of representation, and even sensory images may play an auxiliary role here and there, but this is a far cry from the claim that our thinking is nothing but a series of mental images, subvocal talk, or a pattern of overt behavior. There remains, for one thing, a vast domain of thought, in which images play no role and the sway of the understanding is complete. Most of the propositions in the present work, for instance, belong to this domain.

13. We have come to the realization that our thinking about the individuals of this world is of necessity subjective, that is, affected by the limitations inherent in a human agent. A person can think of, and talk about, an individual only in terms

Propositions

of the descriptions he happens to know. This subjectivity is reinforced by the egocentric way of one's perception and representation of objects in space and time. This limitation is implicitly recognized by our willingness to grant that there are other aspects of the same things, unknown to us but possibly known to others, and to regard the egocentric nature of our spatiotemporal representation as distinct from the "objective" order of things, which might furnish the material for other "subjective" representations in other minds.

Even with respect to such "abstract" things as mathematical objects there is an element of acknowledged subjectivity in our thinking. My concept of a triangle, for instance, never exhausts "the" concept of a triangle, since I do not know all that can be known about that figure. In this case, however, considerations of time and location do not provide an added source of subjectivity.

Thus we are aware of the fact that our thoughts belong to the phenomenal order: inasmuch as they represent the world, they represent it as it appears to us, not as it is in itself. Of course, this very awareness points beyond the phenomenal and gives rise to the idea of objectivity—that is, of a system of "propositions" that transcend the limitations imposed by human ignorance, in particular the subjectivity ("opaqueness") of reference. I submit that the concept of fact (and possibility) corresponds to this idea.

It is well known that facts are like propositions in many respects. For one thing, the grammatical forms we employ in mentioning facts appear to be identical with the ones we use in reproducing statements, beliefs, and so forth; they are nothing but variants of the familiar noun-clause. For instance, the clause *that p* fits into the frames *Joe said . . .* , *John thinks . . .* , and *. . . is a fact* with equal ease. Moreover, in certain

81

cases at least, the fact itself seems to be the object of a performative, as in *Joe has stated the fact that p*, or *What Joe has stated is a fact*.

The curious thing, however, is that although what Joe stated may be a fact, his statement—the product of his stating—cannot be called a fact. Even if true, his statement is not a fact; it only fits (or corresponds to) the facts. This reminds us of the ambiguity in *what the painter paints*: in painting a picture of a rose he is painting a rose. So, in a sense, what he is painting is a rose, yet his painting is not a rose, it is but a picture of a rose. In this light, propositions are like pictures: "We make to ourselves pictures of facts." [12] Indeed, like a picture, a proposition is somebody's creation; propositions, as we remarked above, belong to somebody or other. Facts do not. They are "there," objectively given, to be found or discovered.

14. In particular, there are three notions that explicitly involve the objective realm, the world of facts: truth, causation, and knowledge. It was the idea of referential opacity that first revealed to us the subjectivity of propositions. Correspondingly, we are going to find that the three notions just mentioned all imply, at one point or another, a certain "transparency" of reference.

One important aspect of certain illocutionary acts, and of some mental acts and states, is the dimension of truth. Statements and verdicts (but not orders and promises) and beliefs and opinions (but not wishes and regrets) are true or false. Truth and falsity do not depend upon the maker of the statement or the holder of the belief. Nor do they depend upon other people's statements and opinions. Persuading or converting other people to one's own beliefs will not show their

12 Wittgenstein, *Tractatus*, 2.1.

Propositions

truth; "truth by convention" is a myth. A statement or belief is true if it agrees with what is the case, if it fits the facts. Moreover, in this context, as opposed to indirect discourse, the variety of equivalent referring devices does not matter. If it is true that Ocdipus marricd Jocasta, and Jocasta is his mother, then it must be true that he married his mother. The very concept of referential equivalence depends upon the notion of truth: two devices of reference are equivalent if and only if they are interchangeable in all propositions *salva veritate*.

The proposition that Oedipus married Jocasta is different from the proposition that he married his mother; the fact, on the other hand, that Oedipus married Jocasta cannot be different from the fact that he married his mother. Since truth consists in a conformity with the facts, if these facts were different, then there would be no reason why the truth-values of those two propositions should necessarily be the same. Do not say that since Jocasta is Oedipus' mother, these facts, though different, are necessarily connected. Connected, how? They cannot be true together, because, as I am going to show in the next chapter, facts are not true or false at all. For one thing, what would make a fact true? Correspondence with some "superfact"? And, for another thing, what could be a false fact? The vernacular is very suggestive here: Jocasta is, *in fact* (i.e., regardless of our ways of thinking), the mother of Oedipus.

Next the question arises concerning the possibility of referential equivalence in false propositions. That Napoleon III won the battle of Sedan, and that the last French emperor won the battle of Sedan are two propositions that must be true or false together. As it happens, they are false. Therefore there is no corresponding fact. Nevertheless, one must admit, there is a corresponding possibility; one corresponding possibility, not two.

15. The realm of unrealized possibilities would put a strain on anybody's ontological liberalism, were it not for the fact that we do have the concept of objective (i.e., not thought-dependent) possibility; moreover, we are often actually affected by tenuous entities of this kind. As the fact that my friend is ill may shock or surprise me, so the possibility of his loss may upset or worry me, whereas the same fact and the same possibility may please or delight his enemy. There are not only "propositional actions," such as thinking or saying something, but "propositional passions," such as surprise, shock, and delight. Of course, in all these cases one might also say that it is the thought of my friend's illness, or the idea of his possible demise, that really shocks or upsets me. This, however, does not prove that the fact or possibility in question is a merely subjective, thought-dependent entity. These things are apprehended in the form of a proposition, but this is merely the subjective appearance of an objective reality. Suppose I do not know that my friend is your cousin. Is it true, then, that the illness of your cousin, or the possibility of his death, worries me? Yes and no. Yes, if one focuses one's attention on the fact, the objective element, but no if the subjective appearance, the proposition, is considered. Think of the analogy of sense-perception. Often a particular appearance of a harmless object, a tree or a rock, may frighten even the brave soul. Is it then true that he was frightened by a tree? Yes and no.[13]

A far more important reason for admitting the objective existence of facts at least is derived from the concept of causation. Since I have discussed this topic at least three times be-

---

[13] We often use the word *thought* in a detached sense: not as somebody's thought, but just "the thought." E.g.: "The thought that the earth might move has never occurred to the Mayas." *Thought*, in this Fregean sense, is equivalent to *possibility*.

fore, I here merely summarize the main result by quoting what I called the "transcendental principle of causality": "For every event there is a set of facts, each of them being a necessary condition of the occurrence of that event, and all of them jointly amounting to a sufficient condition." [14] These conditions are viewed as objective facts, not as subjective propositions: causal contexts are notoriously transparent. If the explosion in the tire factory caused the conflagration, and if that factory happens to be the tallest building in town, then it must be the case that the explosion in the tallest building in town caused the conflagration.

Finally, as we are going to see in the next chapter, the analysis of the concept of knowledge, particularly as contrasted with the concept of belief, will lead us once more over the same terrain, giving a more detailed view of the lay of the land and resolving the problems that, no doubt, still remain.

16. Earlier (Chapter III, section 10) I spoke of man as living in two worlds, the world of the body and the world of the mind. As a body, man enters various relationships with parts of the material world: through active and passive physical contact, and through sense-perception, he affects, and is affected by, this environment. These relationships do not, of course, abrogate but presuppose the objective existence of the physical world. The situation is similar in the world of the mind. Man's life, as a thinking thing, is conditioned by the objective realm of facts and possibilities, which are reflected in his mind, imperfectly, and with distortions, in the subjective form of propositions—passively, as in the attitudes of belief; actively, as in the stances of will. This dualism is not complete, however. In

[14] "Causal Relations," *The Journal of Philosophy*, LXIV (1967), 704–713.

this chapter we have come to the realization that this thinking thing must be anchored in space and time, must be tied to a body. For the subjectivity of human thought is not due merely to ignorance, but also to a perspective imposed by a spatiotemporal location.[15]

How, then, can we have the idea of an "objective" proposition, of a "belief," as it were, without the restrictions of a human believer? Because no less is involved in our taking a proposition as representing a fact, which move is required by the notions of truth, causation, and knowledge.

Think of an omniscient being, demon, or god. Since he knows everything, he would not be affected by the subjectivity arising from ignorance or the limitations of a spatiotemporal perspective. He would be able to "see" all things from all possible points of view, that is, according to all possible ways of referring to them. Consequently, there would be no opaqueness, that is, no subjectivity in his "beliefs" at all (he would see the world *"sub specie aeternitatis"*). His mind, then, would comprehend all the facts, everything that is the case, and more: he would know what is not the case, though could be the case; he would know all possibilities (for the world of facts is a subset of the sum total of all possibilities). In imagining such a

15 It is almost superfluous to mention that the doctrine here developed is similar to Leibniz's well-known view. E.g.: "And as the same city looked at from different sides appears entirely different, and is as if multiplied *perspectively*, so also it happens that, as a result of the infinite multitude of simple substances, there are as it were so many universes, which are nevertheless only the perspectives of a single one, according to the different *points of view* of each monad" (*Monadology*, 57; Wiener, p. 544). "Since every monad is in its way a mirror of the universe, . . . there must also be an order in the representative, that is, in the perceptions of the soul, and hence in the body, through which the universe is represented in the soul" (*Ibid.* 63; Wiener, p. 546).

being, we have, of course, reconstructed Kant's "transcendental ideal."

Then forget the demon and retain the facts and possibilities. The "ideal" appears to be the result of an abstraction from the subjectivity of human representation. As the proposition is abstracted from the variety of synonymous linguistic media, so facts (and possibilities) represent a further abstraction, this time from equivalent referring media. In a proposition the referring element has both "sense" and "reference"; on the level of facts the sense drops out and the reference is pure, giving us the ideal of a logically proper name. As the ultimate substratum of an individual (the *materia prima* of the medievals, the "know not what" of Locke) is devoid of all characteristics, so the ideal name of an individual is empty of all connotations.

Mathematical objects, and similar abstract things, have no substratum; consequently with them the element of reference, at least in the final analysis, cannot be distinguished from that of sense. Accordingly, a language without singular terms —that is, a language wholly intelligible—is sufficient in these domains. Human ignorance will show, of course: some people will try to find the largest prime or to square the circle. Their failure, however, is a conceptual matter and is not due to the fact that, say, the largest prime does not happen to exist in some place or other. In mathematics all these notions—reference, fact, possibility, and even truth—apply only in an analogous sense. Unfortunately, I cannot inquire here into these matters in detail.

What I have to consider, however, is an objection arising from the Sapir-Whorf hypothesis of linguistic relativism.[16] Partisans of this view might argue at this point that even the

16 See B. L. Whorf, *Language, Thought and Reality.*

world of facts and possibilities does not depend merely upon the nature of the physical world, but also on the quality of the particular language in which the world is reflected to the group of humans speaking that language. For reasons that ought to be obvious to the reader, I do not accept this theory. Nevertheless I have to grant this much: facts and possibilities do depend upon the conceptual framework of the human mind, which, as I intend to show in Chapter VI, must transcend the idiosyncrasies manifested in particular languages or language groups. Once the world is given, and the human mind is given, the facts and possibilities arise as something objective, that is, as transcending the limitations of individual humans and their tribes. Thus even the "god" of our transcendental ideal is an anthropomorphic one, not surprisingly, since objectivity itself is a human ideal. How the world is *"an Sich,"* or how it appears to a nonhuman observer—thereof, indeed, one must remain silent.

V

On What One Knows[1]

1. I have mentioned in the previous chapter that the same grammatical construction, the familiar noun-clause, is commonly used either to express a proposition or to denote a fact. Yet, as the same chapter shows, there is a very important difference between propositions and facts, corresponding to the difference between the subjective and the objective dimensions of the mental world. It would be surprising, therefore, if our language were as irresponsive to this distinction as the superficial identity of the noun-clauses seems to suggest. This, fortunately, is not the case. A careful analysis will show that noun-clauses are demonstrably ambiguous in this respect, and that, at least in their underlying structure, they discriminate between contexts implying subjective and objective employment.

---

[1] An earlier version of this chapter was read at the Minnesota Center for the Philosophy of Science in 1968, and will be published, with the comments of Professor Bruce Aune and my reply, in a forthcoming volume of the *Minnesota Studies in the Philosophy of Science.*

Res Cogitans

The concept of knowledge, I have claimed, as much as the concepts of truth and causality, involves the objective domain. Moreover, since it is, unlike the other two, a psychological notion, I propose to approach the problem of the ambiguity of noun-clauses as they occur with the verb *know* and, for contrast, with the verb *believe*. This study, then, will not only reinforce the findings of the previous chapter, but will also provide a sample of the detail work still needed for a full understanding of the variety of speech-acts, mental acts, and mental states.

2.   In spite of the repeated efforts of so many philosophers— since the time Plato wrote his *Theaetetus* to the present day— to clarify the concept of knowledge, the results achieved are by no means satisfactory. There are a number of fairly obvious features of this concept which are simply ignored by most philosophers, and which, accordingly, cannot be squared with the prevailing theories.

The most persistent, and still dominant, line of analysis tries to understand knowledge in terms of belief, true belief, true belief with adequate evidence, grounds, accessibility, or some other, often very elaborately and ingeniously stated condition. Whether such a claim is advanced as a reduction, or merely as a list of necessary conditions, I think it is still misleading and prejudices the issue. For it is taken for granted by the proponents of this view that knowledge (at least in the sense of *knowing that*) can have the same object as belief—that is, that it is possible to believe and to know exactly the same thing.

This, it seems to me, is a highly questionable assumption. Granted, it is nonsense to say that one knows that *p* but does not believe it. It need not follow, however, that in this case one must believe that *p*. What is known may be something

On What One Knows

that cannot be believed or disbelieved at all. In other words, the incongruity of the sentence *I know that p but I do not believe it* may be due not to an implied inconsistency but to a category confusion similar to the one embedded in the sentence *I have a house but I do not covet it*. As one cannot be said to covet or fail to covet one's own property, it may be that one cannot believe or disbelieve what one knows. Again, from the fact that what one knows cannot be false, it does not follow that it must be true and hence that knowledge must entail true belief, if what is known is not a thing to which truth and falsity apply. A picture may be faithful or not faithful, not its object; yet it is the conformity with the object that makes a picture faithful. In a similar way, conformity with things known may render beliefs true, without these things being true themselves. At this point I offer these considerations as mere possibilities; the task remains to justify the analogies I have suggested.

In recent years our comprehension of the concept of knowledge has been enriched by Ryle's distinction between knowing that and knowing how and Austin's recognition of the performative aspect of the verb *to know*. These are valuable insights, but the features they single out do not account for the essence of the concept. Knowing that is distinct from knowing how, as it is distinct from knowing who, what, when, where, why, or whether, and from knowing a story, a house, or one's friend. What is it, beyond the use of the same word, that is common to all these cases, or, at least, what are the interlocking similarities that would constitute a family resemblance? As for the performative aspect, its presence is not sufficient to make *know* a bona fide illocutionary verb; the intuition, moreover, that tells us that this verb, unlike, say, *declare* or *promise*, denotes a mental state and not a speech-act, is too strong to be ignored.

Res Cogitans

In any case, the performative aspect hardly applies beyond the domain of knowing that; consequently it too fails to account for the unity, no matter how loose, of this concept.

3. What do you know? Things of surprisingly many kinds. There are only a few verbs (among them another philosophers' darling, *see*) that display a similar versatility. In the previous section I have mentioned in passing the main categories of the possible verb-objects of *know*. The verb *believe*, which is supposed to help us in our task, is much more restricted. In comparing these two verbs, which is indeed helpful, I shall begin at a rather unsophisticated level, restricting my observations to what some grammarians would call the surface structure of the noun-phrases involved. As we go on, the very nature of the investigation will force us to break through the crust and reveal more and more of the underlying structure.

There is a domain which appears to be shared by both verbs. This comprises the familiar *that*-clauses—that is, nominals formed simply by prefixing *that* to an unaltered sentence. *I know that* and *I believe that* can be followed by any declarative sentence regardless of tense, modality, or structural variation. There is, on the other hand, a domain which is wholly owned by *know* to the exclusion of *believe*. One can be said to know, but not believe, birds and flowers, houses and cars, wines and detergents, cities and deserts. Practically any original noun will do, with or without such adjuncts as the relative clause and its derivatives. Names and other phrases denoting people also qualify, of course, but at this point *believe* re-enters the picture. After all, you can say that you believe Jane as well as that you know Jane. Needless to say that these two assertions have very little to do with one another. Believing a person may require knowing him (to some extent), but knowing him certainly does not entail believing him: the chief reason for not believing Jane may be the fact that you know her too well. At this point the reader will protest: "But, of course, *know* and *believe* operate in totally different ways in *these* cases!" In other words, the reader wants to peek below the surface. For the time being I shall thwart his desire.

There is another group of nouns appropriate to either *know* or *believe*, and which creates a similar situation. I think of *story, tale, explanation, theory, testimony*, and, perhaps, *opinion, suspicion, assumption*, and the like. All these things can be known or believed; but even if they are known, the question of belief remains open. It is perfectly normal to say, for instance, "I know the story but I do not believe it." The reader may again protest that this is all very obvious. I shall once more resist the urge to dig deeper, however, for we do not yet know enough to see the reasons for the protest.

In connection with Ryle's *knowing how*, I have mentioned the other *wh*-forms, such as *what, when*, and *why*, that can introduce the verb-object of *know*. This move, in general, fails with *believe*; whereas one can know where the treasure is hidden, one cannot believe where the treasure is hidden. There is one exception to this incompatibility, and that concerns *what*. I may believe what you said as I may know what you said. Clearly, the relation of these two claims is similar to the one just encountered between knowing and believing stories or people. The knowledge of what one said does not imply belief, but the belief of what one said presupposes the knowledge of what one said. Since the word *what*, unlike the words figuring in the previous examples, is a purely grammatical word, we can nourish the hope that in this case we shall be able to "disambiguate" the offending phrase on syntactical grounds alone, and then apply the result to the previous contexts to relieve the reader's frustration.[2]

4. There are whats and whats. Consider the following three sentences:

(1) Joe lost his watch
(2) I found what he lost
(3) I know what he lost.

Together, (1) and (2) entail that I found Joe's watch; (1) and (3), however, do not entail that I know his watch. *What* in (2) amounts to *that which* (or *the thing which*)—that is, to a demonstrative pronoun (or a dummy noun) followed by the relative pronoun beginning a relative clause. As always, such a clause depends upon a noun-sharing between two ingredient sentences. The derivation of (2) can be sketched as follows:

(4) I found (a watch)   (4a) He lost (a watch)
(5) I found (the watch)   (5a) which he lost
(6) I found that   (6a) which he lost
(7)   I found what he lost

(5a) is a relative clause obtained by replacing *a watch* by *which*. Since the clause is taken to be identifying, *watch* in (5) obtains *the*.[3] In (6) *that* replaces *the watch*. Finally, in (7), *that which* is contracted into *what*.

What in (3) cannot be analyzed into *that which*. It is not

---

[2] By the way, a closer look at *that* and *what* will relieve another frustration, voiced by Austin in these words: "My explanation is very obscure, like those of all grammar books on 'that' clauses: compare their even worse explanation of 'what' clauses" (*How to Do Things with Words*, p. 71, n. 1).

[3] Concerning relative clauses and the definite article, see my *Adjectives and Nominalizations*, Chapter I.

the watch he lost that I claim to know, but rather that it is a watch that he lost, although I put my claim in an indefinite form. *What he lost,* in this case, has nothing to do with a relative clause; it is a sentence nominalization on a par with *who lost the watch, when he lost it, how he lost it,* and the like. This nominalization operates by replacing a noun-phrase or an adverbial phrase in the original sentence by *wh* plus the appropriate pro-morpheme. Since the same replacement is used in the corresponding question transformations, the resulting noun-phrases are traditionally called "indirect questions." This name is misleading, however. Granted that after *wonder,* or some such verb, these nominals retain their interrogative flavor, but this is not true after *know, tell, learn,* or *realize.* This becomes clear as we contrast the sentences:

> I wonder what he lost, (namely) a watch *or* a ring *or* . . .
> I know what he lost, namely a watch.

The strings following *namely* are not interchangeable. It is easy to restore the underlying sentences from which these two are derived by the removal of redundancy. They are:

> I wonder what he lost, namely (I wonder whether he lost) a watch or a ring or . . .
> I know what he lost, namely (I know that he lost) a watch.

It appears, therefore, that the *what*-clause after *wonder* comes via an earlier step in the process of nominalization, that is

> *whether* he lost a watch *or* a ring *or* . . .

whereas the *what*-clause after *know* comes via a different intermediate step, to wit,

> *that* he lost a watch.

The same ambiguity can be shown with respect to other *wh*-forms such as *who, when,* and *why*. Those coming through *whether* can indeed be called indirect questions, but the ones derived from the *that*-form should rather be called indirect, or indefinite, *claims*. Accordingly, the correct analysis for (3) will be the following:

(8) I know . . .   (8a) He lost (a watch)
(9) I know . . .   (9a) that he lost (a watch)
(10) I know . . .   (10a) what he lost
(11)   I know what he lost.

To repeat, (10a) is not a relative clause but a *wh*-nominal formed out of (9a). The dots in (8)–(10) indicate the "noun-gap," characteristic of container sentences, which is to be filled by an appropriate nominal.[4]

It is interesting to note that *wh*-clauses after the negation of *know* do not come through *that* but *whether*. The correct analysis of, say,

I do not know what he ate

and of

I do not know where he went

will show

I do not know whether he ate . . . or . . . or . . .

and

I do not know whether he went to . . . or to . . . or to . . .

rather than

[4] *Ibid.*, Chapter II.

96

On What One Knows

I do not know that he ate (fish)

and

I do not know that he went to (Paris).

This is interesting linguistically: it shows that the negation precedes the nominalization in the generative process.

Wh-nominals are not confined to the object position; they can occur as subjects too:

Who killed her is uncertain
Why she went there is a mystery.

This possibility permits us to draw another interesting comparison between the structures underlying *what he lost.*

(12) What he lost is a watch
(13) What he lost is a mystery.

(12) is contracted from

That which he lost is a watch

which is an extraction transform of

He lost a watch.

On the other hand, (13) is certainly no transform of

He lost a mystery.

5. These facts enable us to explain the ambiguity of *what he said* in the sentences:

(14) I believe what he said
(15) I know what he said.

Believe cannot take *wh*-nominals, consequently the analysis of (14) cannot follow the pattern of (3). The correct analogy is

Res Cogitans

provided by (2): the object of *believe* is a pronoun (or dummy noun) followed by a relative clause. In full:

(a) I believe (that *p*)   He said (that *p*)
    I believe that   which he said
        I believe what he said.

Roughly, the object of your saying and my believing is the same thing. Not so in (15). The object of my knowledge is not the object of your saying (*that p*), but, obviously, an indefinite version of *that you said that p*. Thus the derivation matches (8)–(11) above:

(b) I know . . .   He said (that *p*)
    I know . . .   that he said (that *p*)
    I know . . .   what he said
        I know what he said.

The possibility of *believing what* (= *that which* or *the thing which*) is restricted to "things" that can be objects of belief. For this reason, such sentences as

  * I believe what he lost

are ruled out: the relevant co-occurrence sets of *believe* and *lose*, unlike those of *believe* and *say*, do not overlap. Roughly speaking, *believe* demands *that*-clauses, but *lose* requires object nouns. If so, the intelligent reader will ask, what saves (15) from being given the relative-clause interpretation in addition to the other one, and from consequent ambiguity, since the object range of *say* and of *know* widely overlap in the domain of *that*-clauses? Twist as we might, (15) is not ambiguous. It seems, therefore, that the *that*-clauses following *say* are different from the *that*-clauses following *know*. And since the former are of the kind which is compatible with *believe*, it seems to follow

98

that the *that*-clauses after *know* are different from the *that*-clauses after *believe*—that *know* and *believe* cannot have identical objects at all. We shall see that this is indeed the case.

To emphasize the point, consider another verb, *tell*. In this case, the phrase *knowing what he told* (*somebody*) is indeed ambiguous. Although the sentence

> I know what he told you

most likely will be interpreted in the sense of the *wh*-nominal (*I know that he told you that p*), I can elicit the other interpretation by saying, for instance,

> I already knew what he just told you.

Here I claim to know that *p* (which he just told you). One cannot play the same trick with *say*. The sentence,

> I already knew what he just said (to you)

is substandard, and the improved version,

> I already knew what he would say . . .

once more selects the path of the *wh*-nominal. *Know*, therefore, is capable of absorbing the dummy for a *that*-clause, provided this latter is of the right kind. Now *tell*, but not *say*, seems to provide such. What, then, is the difference between *say* and *tell* in this respect? I shall take up this problem later on. For the time being, let us remember that just as there are whats and whats, so are there thats and thats.

6. It is time to return to the problem of knowing and believing people and stories. First I shall consider belief. It is clear that a sentence such as

> (16) I believe Jane

99

must be elliptical. For one thing, the breakdown of two common transformations (passive and extraction) shows that the sentence is "abnormal" for some reason or other:

> *Jane is believed by me
> ?It is Jane that I believe.

Intuition tells us that what (16) means is this:

> I believe what Jane said (would or will say).

What, of course, is *that which*. This intuition mirrors a general deletion pattern that tends to substitute the subject of saying or doing something for the saying or doing itself:

> I refuted him (what he claimed)
> I understood him (what he said)
> I imitated him (what he did)
> I heard him (his voice)

and so on. In a similar way, the sentence

> I believe his story (explanation, etc.)

is but an ellipsis of

> I believe what his story (contains, says, etc.).

The verbs in the parentheses are not to be taken too seriously. They are but idiomatic crutches to facilitate the move to the deep structure. What is essential is that this latter contains the elements,

> I believe that p

and

> His story (explanation, etc.) is that p

and that the two are fused into a relative clause construction by virtue of the identical noun-phrase (*that p*).

On What One Knows

It appears, therefore, that all occurrences of *believe* (I am not considering believing *in* somebody or something) can be re duced to *believe that*.

Nevertheless, this verb retains some latitude, inasmuch as it can take substitutes for the *that*-clauses (*it, thing, what*). This, interestingly enough, is not true of a cognate verb, *think*. This one takes *that*-clauses without discrimination, but refuses substitutes. One can answer, for instance, *I believe it* but not *I think it*, and owing to the exclusion of dummies, it is impossible to think a person, a story, or what one said. This point is obviously connected with the fact that the appropriate pro-morpheme after *think* is the pro-adverb *so* rather than the pronoun *it: I think so. Believe* can take either, yet with a different emphasis: *I believe so* deals with a proposition on its own merits; *I believe it* reflects upon what someone else has said. *Know*, incidentally, hardly takes *so*. Later on I shall return to this difference between *think* and *believe*.

What, then, about knowing a story, an explanation, or other things of this sort? Knowing these things differs from believing them in exactly the same way as knowing what one said differs from believing what one said. Accordingly, knowing a story is but shorthand for knowing what the story is or how the story goes. And, as the parallel with *how* clearly indicates, this *what* is not *that which*. The same goes for tales, reasons, explanations, excuses, and theories offered by somebody or other. Incidentally, whereas these things, as we recall, can also be believed (but what a difference!), poems, jokes, names, foreign words, tongue twisters, and the like can be known, but not believed. The reason is obvious. The possibility of believing, say, a story is tied to the existence of the sentence

The story is that *p*

which makes the relative-clause inclusion possible. Poems,

tongue twisters, and the like, on the other hand, cannot be reproduced in *that*-clauses; consequently there is no way of connecting them with *believe*. Nothing prevents their being known, however. Knowing a poem, for instance, is knowing how it goes, or, if one is more ambitious, knowing how it is to be understood, interpreted, and what not.

The availability of the inexhaustible variety of *wh*-nominals the verb *know* can take makes it a relatively easy matter to explicate one element of the concept of knowing such things as a person, a house, a car, or a city. What, for instance, can you possibly mean when you say that you know Jane? There is a "minimal" sense of this claim, which is satisfied if you have ever met her in the flesh and, perhaps, talked to her. Yet, in spite of such an encounter, you may still insist that you do not know her ("I have met her, but I do not know her at all"). What is it that you disclaim in this case? What would be knowing her in this fuller sense? Well, it is an open-ended affair. It might be merely knowing what her full name is, where she comes from, what she does for a living, and other particulars of this sort. If you know her better, if you "really" know her, then you know what she thinks, how she feels about various matters, what she would do if . . . ; consequently you know how to treat her, and the like.

Knowing all these things *about* Jane will not, however, normally entitle one to claim that one knows her without the personal acquaintance previously mentioned. I do not know Mao Tse-tung, although I know many things about him. Yet, some latitude remains in this respect. Churchill could have truthfully said, during World War II, "I know Hitler; he would destroy his country rather than surrender," even if he had never met Hitler in the flesh. But, one might argue, they at least had some dealings with one another, which is not true of Mao and me.

On What One Knows

Again, the sentence *I used to know him many years ago* suggests an interruption of contact rather than of the flow of relevant information.[5]

Mutatis mutandis, the same analysis works for knowing houses, cars, cities, and the like. Does the armchair geographer who knows a great deal about Lhasa know Lhasa? Does the little old lady from Dubuque who spent two days in Paris with a guided tour know Paris?

I suspect that the requirement of contact (acquaintance) is a hangover from the ancient sense of *know,* according to which knowing, say, pain and misery meant having these things, and which sense is also reflected in the phrase *carnal knowledge.* We are going to see, toward the end of this chapter, that this element of contact with something actually "there" still pertains to the concept of knowledge throughout the entire domain of its application.[6]

The phrase I just used, *knowing how to treat her,* represents a new construction which I did not mention before among the possible objects of *know.* It is by no means restricted to *knowing how.* I know whom to blame, what to do, where to look, and when to stop in many situations. The transformational origin of these phrases is quite clear. The infinitive, to V +, is generally used in sentence nominalizations to code a noun-sharing between the subject of the nominalized sentence and either the subject or the direct object of the container sentence, provided there is a modal verb in the former sentence. These features can be brought out with greater or lesser grammaticality in appropriate paraphrases; for example:

[5] I am indebted to Professor Paul Ziff for a clearer perception of these two aspects of knowing a person.

[6] In many languages there are two distinct words corresponding to *know,* one for noun-clause objects and the other for simple noun-objects (*wissen-kennen, savoir-connaître,* etc.).

Res Cogitans

I decided to go   —I decided that *I should* go
I persuaded him to go—I persuaded *him* that *he should* go
I know where to go   —*I* know where *I should* go
I know how to solve —*I* know how *I can* solve the prob-
the problem   lem

and so forth. As we see, there is nothing special about *knowing how to*.

Reviewing our results, we find that the acquaintance-sense aside, all verb-objects of *know*, other than the *that*-clause, can be reduced to *wh*-nominals. Now these, themselves, are nothing but indefinite versions of *that*-clauses, formed, as we recall, by replacing a noun-phrase or an adverbial phrase in the sentence following *that* by *wh* plus the appropriate pro-morpheme. Consequently, whenever I claim that I know *wh* . . . , I guarantee that I could make another claim in which the *wh*-nominal is replaced by a corresponding *that*-clause. It makes perfect sense to say that I know what he did but will not tell you; to say, on the other hand, that I know what he did but could not possibly tell you is absurd.

It will be objected here that in some cases of knowing how it is impossible to tell, in words, what one knows. I know how to tie a necktie, but I could not tell you in words alone. I grant this, but point out that this situation is possible with nearly all the *knowing wh* forms. I know what coffee tastes like, what the color magenta looks like, where it itches on my back, when I should stop drinking, how the coastline of Angola runs, but I could not tell you in words alone. I must have, however, some other means to supplement words: pointing; offering a sample, a sketch, a demonstration; or saying "now." By these means I can tell you, or show you, what I know: I know that magenta looks like this (offering a sample), that it itches here (point-

ing), that I should stop drinking now. The need for supplementing words with nonlinguistic media affects knowing how, and
knowing *wh* in general, exactly because it affects the corresponding knowing that.[7]

I leave it to the imagination of the reader to account, along
similar lines, for the meaning of such phrases as *knowing geography*, *knowing Aristotle*, and *knowing Russian*.

7. In the previous section we have concluded that the basic
form of the verb-object for both *believe* and *know* is the *that*-
clause. Yet, at the beginning of this chapter, I suggested that
these verbs cannot have the same verb-object. These two claims
need not conflict, of course, if *that*-clauses can be ambiguous.
And, indeed, we have already encountered one reason for thinking that they are: roughly, the object of *say*, a *that*-clause, can
be the object of *believe* but not the object of *know*. In this section I shall present the remainder of the evidence that points in
the same direction.

My main argument involves a group of nouns that are normally joined to *that*-clauses by means of the copula; for example:

> His suggestion is that *p*
> That *p* is his prediction
> That *p* is a fact
> The cause of the phenomenon is that *p*.

Clearly, there is a need to subdivide this class. Words like *suggestion, prediction, statement, confession, testimony*, and *ex-*

[7] In view of what we discovered about the role of the imagination in
certain mental states in the previous chapter, it is not surprising that in
many cases of saying something we make use of such nonlinguistic media
as pointing, drawing, and imitating. As understanding often involves imagining, so saying often involves showing.

cuse on the one hand, and *belief, opinion, assumption, view, theory,* and *suspicion* on the other, are derivatives either of performative verbs or of verbs of mental states. This is shown in the typical transformation exemplified by

He suggested that *p*—His suggestion is that *p*
He suspects that *p* —His suspicion is that *p*.

The *that*-clause, accordingly, is tied to a person, and this tie is specified by the words just listed, which I shall call "subjective" P-nouns. This class is to be distinguished from the class of "objective" P-nouns, which includes *fact, cause, result, outcome, upshot,* and a few others. Facts, causes, and the like do not belong to anybody, and the transformation just given has no parallel. Some P-nouns cross the line—for example, *reason* and *explanation*. One can speak of Joe's reason or Joe's explanation versus *the* reason or *the* explanation.

These two groups behave quite differently with respect to *know* and *believe*. Subjective P-nouns can follow either verb, but the analyses of the resulting sentences go along quite different lines. If, for instance, someone's prediction is that *p*, then believing his prediction is believing that *p*; knowing that prediction, however, never means knowing that *p*, but rather knowing what that prediction is—that is, knowing that the prediction is that *p*. It appears, therefore, that *that*-clauses marked by subjective P-nouns are per se compatible with *believe* but not with *know*. The latter verb cannot take these *that*-clauses except in a roundabout way, via the *wh*-nominal.

In view of what we found before, it is easy to give the analyses of the two sentences involved:

(c) I believe (that *p*)   His prediction is (that *p*)
    I believe that   which is his prediction

106

On What One Knows

I believe what is his prediction
I believe his prediction.

(d) I know . . .   His prediction is (that p)

I know . . .   that his prediction is (that p)

I know . . .   what his prediction is

I know his prediction.

The sentence with *believe* cannot follow the second pattern, since, as we recall, this verb cannot take *wh*-nominals. What is more interesting, and indeed decisive, is that the sentence with *know* does not conform to the first pattern. The clause *that p*, insofar as it is marked as a prediction—that is, as something subjective, something produced by an illocutionary act—is not an appropriate object of *know*.

The situation is quite different with objective P-nouns. They naturally follow *know*, but only with great strain *believe*. You may know the facts about the crime, the cause of the explosion, the result of too much publicity and the outcome of the trial. But what could possibly be meant by such a sentence as *I believe the cause of the explosion* or *I believe the outcome of the trial?* It might be objected that results are said to be believed or disbelieved: it makes sense to say *I do not believe the results of the autopsy.* We quickly realize, however, that in this case one speaks of the results submitted by some experts; they are "their" results. If no human authorship is involved, then believing or disbelieving results is impossible; it is nonsense to say, for instance, *I do not believe the results of the inflation.* In a similar way one may believe or not believe the "facts" submitted by the police, but not the facts about the crime.

The analysis of a sentence like *I know the cause of the explosion* is interesting. It goes via the *wh*-nominal: *I know what is the cause of the explosion,* that is, *I know that the cause of the explosion is that p.* This, of course, entails that I know that *p.* If I know that the cause of the explosion was the overheating of the wire (that the wire got overheated), then I know that the wire got overheated. The words *cause, result, outcome,* and so forth are relative, inasmuch as they are followed by a genitive structure in non-elliptical sentences: causes, results, outcomes, and the like are causes, results, and outcomes of something or other. Hence knowing the cause of the explosion is not merely knowing that *p,* which is the cause, but knowing that that *p* is the cause, that is, knowing what is the cause.

Facts are not relative in this respect. Consequently these two paths merge into one. Indeed, *I know that that p is a fact* or *I know for a fact that p* are but emphatic forms of *I know that p.* Of course one can relate facts to something or other and say, for example, *I know the facts about the crime,* which means *I know what are the facts about the crime,* that is, *I know that the facts about the crime are that p and that q, etc.* This, naturally, entails that I know that *p,* that *q,* and so on.

At this point we should recall what we said about the relevant difference between *say* and *tell.* If you said that *p,* and I believe what you said, then I believe that *p:* knowing what you said, however, does not mean knowing that *p,* but knowing that you said that *p. Tell* works differently: if you told me that *p,* then knowing what you told me may mean, in a suitable context, that I know that *p.* This seems to suggest that *tell,* but not *say,* is an objective P-verb. It is not surprising to find, therefore, that one can tell, but not say, the facts about the crime, the cause of the explosion, the outcome of the trial, and so forth. *Tell* belongs to the family of *know; say* to that of *believe.*

The urge to find symmetries makes us ask why it is that one cannot say suggestions, predictions, opinions, and the like. The answer is simple. *Say,* like *think,* can take *that*-clauses, but not their substitutes: you may believe that *p,* think that *p,* or say that *p;* but if I predict that *p,* then you may believe my prediction, but not think or say my prediction.

But—it may be objected—I can surely tell you my prediction or opinion, and this move seems to cross the line between the subjective and the objective. No more, I reply, than knowing opinions or predictions. The *wh*-nominal bridges over the gap. Telling your prediction or knowing your prediction is telling, or knowing, what that prediction is (and *what,* here, is not *that which*). Telling your prediction is not the same thing as predicting or making a prediction. A prediction is a subjective entity. That one has made a prediction, however, is something objective; it may be a fact.

Wh-nominals in general belong to the objective domain. We have seen that they are compatible with *know* but not with *believe.* Similarly they can follow *tell* but hardly *say.* I can tell you where I went yesterday, what I did there, and why. Putting *say* for *tell* in such a context will yield ungrammaticality or at least substandard speech:

> ?He said where he went (. . . what he did . . . why he did it).

Notice, however, that negation changes the picture. There is nothing wrong with the sentence

> He did not say where he went (. . . what he did . . . why he did it).

We know, of course (from Section 4, above), that the presence of negation means that the subsequent *wh*-clause is to be derived not from *that p* but rather from *whether p or q or.* . . . It seems, therefore, that such *wh*-clauses are not objective in our sense. Yet *know* takes them, as we recall, at least in its negative form. Consequently negation must strip *know* from its objective force. Is this the reason for the oddity of sentences like

?I do not know that Joe stole the watch

in which the quality of the clause is left up in the air?

A comparison with P-nouns will round out the picture. Sentences such as

*His suspicion is why she did it

and

*Who killed her is my opinion

are ungrammatical. On the other hand, it is easy to pair *wh*-clauses with objective P-nouns:

What he did was the result of despair
How he said it was the cause of the scandal.

It will be helpful to consider a very common verb, *state*, at this point. From our present point of view it is like *tell*, rather than *say*, since obviously one can state a fact or the cause, result, or explanation of something or other. What one states, therefore, is something objective. One's statement, on the other hand, is not. For whereas what one states may be a fact, one's statement, even if true, is never a fact. Accordingly, knowing your statement cannot be anything but knowing what the statement is; knowing what you stated, however, may amount to knowing that *p*, which you stated. Believing your statement, on the other hand, necessarily means believing that *p*, which you stated.

On What One Knows

A little exercise for amusement's sake. What do the following sentences mean?

(17)   I believe what you believe.
(18)   I know what you believe.
(19)   *I believe what you know.
(20)   I know what you know.

The first, (17), means that you and I share a set of beliefs; (18) means that I know what your beliefs are; (19) is deviant; and (20) is ambiguous: it means either that I know what it is that you know, or (with a stress on *you*) that you and I are both acquainted with the same relevant set of facts.

All these differences can readily be accounted for by the following simple hypothesis. There are two kinds of *that*-clauses, the subjective and the objective. They are distinct because, first, they have entirely different co-occurrence restrictions: one kind fits subjective P-nouns and subjective verbs such as *say* and *believe*, the other kind fits objective P-nouns and such objective verbs as *tell* and *know*; second, their transformational potential is different: objective *that*-clauses are open to the *wh*-nominalization, but subjective ones are not. Thus we see that the seemingly trivial and unexplainable "accident" of grammar that, for instance, it is possible for me to know what you ate, but not to believe what you ate, is, in fact, an important clue to the discovery of a fundamental distinction in linguistic structure and in our conceptual framework.

We have seen that *that*-clauses (or their pronoun substitutes) are incompatible with certain contexts as a result of their being embedded in a more immediate context. Since the incompatibility works both ways, we have to assume that the immediate context imprints a mark on the clause, and this mark, subjective or objective, then decides its further cooccurrence restrictions and its transformational behavior with respect to the *wh*-nominalization. Take the phrase *believing what one knows.* Since *believe* rejects *wh*-nominals, the *what* must be *that which.* *That* is a pronoun substituting for a *that*-clause governed by the objective verb *know,* which clause, accordingly, bears an objective mark. This, however, precludes the context *believe.* The phrase, therefore, is ungrammatical; one cannot possibly believe what one knows.

8. Thus far, surprisingly enough in a discussion of knowledge and belief, we have barely mentioned truth and falsity. What we have just said about subjective and objective P-nouns and other propositional containers makes it possible to fill this gap. If one asks what terms paradigmatically cooccur with *true* or *false,* the answer will be the sets of subjective P-nouns: *statement, assertion, testimony,* and the like on the one hand, and *belief, assumption, suspicion,* and the like on the other. Turning to objective P-nouns, we find that although the adjective *true* can be ascribed to them, the resulting compounds require a rather special interpretation. Compare, for instance, *true statement* and *true result.* The analysis of the former phrase is simple and straightforward: a true statement is a statement which is true. The phrase *true result,* however, suggests a different interpretation: a true result is not a result which is true, but something which is truly ("really") the result of something or other. In this sense *true* (like *real*) contrasts not with *false* but with *alleged.* In the same way, the true facts of the case will be contrasted with the alleged facts, true causes with alleged causes, and so forth. In all these contexts *true* can be replaced by *real* without any loss of meaning. *False,* moreover, hardly applies at all; what would a false fact, false cause, or

false result be? Of course, we know from elsewhere that *true* in this adverbial sense is not the opposite of *false*: such phrases as *true fish* or *true North* do not have *false fish* or *false North* as opposites; nor, for that matter, do *false teeth* and *false hair* have *true teeth* and *true hair* for opposites. To argue, therefore, that since there are no false facts, false causes, or false results, all facts, causes, and results must be true, is to commit the same blunder as to conclude that since there are no false fish all fish must be true, or to insist that all hair must be false, since true hair does not exist. Insofar as *true* is opposed to *false* (i.e., is used in an adjectival sense), facts and causes, results and outcomes, are neither true nor false.

We have found, however, that it is exactly these things that are the immediate objects of knowledge. It follows, then, that what is known is not something that can be true or false. What I say or what I believe is true or false, not what I know.

"But surely"—you object—"what I know must be so, must be the case, or even must be the truth. Now do these phrases not mean the same thing as *must be true?*" No, they do not. Consider, once more, the verb *state*. We have shown that the two derivatives, *his statement* and *what he stated* are very different. The former belongs to the subjective domain: his statement may be true, but his statement cannot be a fact. What he stated, however, can be; people often state facts. And, I add now, what he stated may be so, may be the case, or may be the truth. His statement, on the other hand is never the case or the truth. For the same reason, whereas it is possible to ask somebody to tell the truth or tell what is the case, it is not possible to ask people to say the truth or say what is the case. *Tell*, as we recall, is an objective verb, *say* a subjective one.

The phrases *is so*, *is the case*, and *is the truth* are near synonyms for *is a fact*. The phrase *is true*, on the other hand, does not belong to this set. The thing which is true is not a fact; it only fits the facts, corresponds to what is the case, and, perhaps, agrees with the truth. Consequently, what I believe or what I say may fit the facts, in which case it is true; or it may fail to fit the facts, in which case it is false. What I know, however, is the fact itself, not something that merely corresponds, or fails to correspond, to the facts.

"We make to ourselves pictures of facts." [8] We form, conceive, or adopt beliefs, opinions, and the like. And we issue such pictures for the benefit of others in making statements and suggestions, in giving testimonies, descriptions, and so forth. These are subjective things, human creations; they belong to people: we speak of Joe's beliefs or Jane's statements. Facts, results, and causes are objective: they do not belong to anybody. They are "there" to be found, located, or discovered.

A picture is affected by the imperfections of the painter. Accordingly, beliefs, statements, and other subjective things, even when true, bear the marks of human ignorance: they represent the facts from a certain point of view, in a given perspective. This, as we know from the previous chapter, is manifested in the referential opaqueness of such contexts. Even if it is true that Joe believes that A. S. Onassis married Jacqueline Kennedy, it may be false that he believes that Onassis married the widow of the thirty-fifth President of the U.S.A. Yet these two possible beliefs are true together, because they correspond to the same fact. Given this, we are faced with a serious difficulty. If the object of knowledge is not a subjective replica, but the objective fact itself, as we have claimed, then why is it that not only belief contexts, but also knowledge contexts are referentially opaque? For even if Joe knows that Onassis has mar-

8 Wittgenstein, *Tractatus*, 2.1.

ried Jacqueline Kennedy, it is possible that he does not know that Onassis married the widow of the thirty-fifth President of the U.S.A.

This is a very difficult problem, the solution of which requires the utmost care. Let us return to the picture analogy. Given two pictures of the same thing, say of a rose, my claim that I see this or that picture of the rose does not entail that I see the rose itself. I do, of course, see the rose "in the picture," but seeing something "in the picture" is not the same thing as seeing something *in rerum natura.* Therefore, seeing two pictures of the same thing does not entail seeing the same thing. Now consider seeing the rose itself from two points of view. Do I see the same thing? Yes and no. Yes, if I focus my attention on the object seen; no, if I focus my attention on the aspect (appearance) presented to me in the two glances.

I claim that the situation is similar with respect to belief *versus* knowledge. Two persons may hold different beliefs mirroring the same fact; they have, as it were, different pictures of it. If, however, two persons know the same fact, what they know, in one sense, will be the same thing, although what they know may appear to them in different perspectives. The person who knows that Onassis married Jacqueline Kennedy and the person who knows that Onassis married the widow of the late President, without either of them knowing that Jacqueline is that widow, know the same fact, namely *whom Onassis married.* A parallel move, as we recall, is impossible with *believe.* I cannot claim that two persons having beliefs that mirror the same fact, but which differ in the referential apparatus, have the same belief—for example, in our case, that they both believe *whom Onassis married.* The *wh*-nominal transcends referential opaqueness. It is not surprising, therefore, that its application is restricted to objective contexts. The possibility of *wh*-nominalization marks the objective domain of the language.[9]

9. Now the intuitive pieces fall into a consistent pattern. The widely different ways in which we think of knowledge and belief, the difference in their conceptual setting, enhances the importance of the grammatical distinctions just established. I shall select a few salient points for brief discussion, but the list could be continued and the details worked out to the extent of one's patience and curiosity.

I begin with the well known difference in the form of the relevant questions: *Why do you believe . . . ?* and *How do you know . . . ?* *Why* demands reasons, but *how* asks about the key to an achievement. Forming a belief, like painting a picture, or imagining something, is a human act, which can be recommended or discouraged (*You ought to* [or *should not*] *believe it*), praised or censured (*. . . reasonable or foolish belief*), and for which one can and should have reasons. One does not say, on the other hand, that one has reasons for what one knows. Knowing something is not the kind of thing a man can choose to do, believing something very often is. One may try to believe, but not to know. We may, of course, try to learn or find out things, and for doing or not doing these actions one might have reasons, and might incur praise or blame, not

9 The restriction imposed by the *wh*-nominal is so strong that I cannot say, under the penalty of ungrammaticality, things like, "I believe where the treasure is hidden," even if, semantically, this is exactly what I want to say (e.g.: I believe that the treasure is in the second cave; I want you to know that I have an idea where it is; I do not want to tell you yet— till you promise a share, etc.). What *can* I say? "I think (or believe) I know where it is. . . ." *Know* here is a grammatical dummy used to crack the protective shield of the *wh*-nominal.

directly for the resulting knowledge or ignorance. If belief is like forming an image in one's mind, knowledge is like seeing what there is in reality. As looking is a voluntary action, but seeing is not, so trying to find out something is subject to the will, but knowing is not. The relevant question, *How do you know* . . . ? asks for the secret of a success; more often than not for the source of the claimed enlightenment: how did you find out, "whence" do you know? [10]

Then compare wanting to know with wanting to believe something or other. The first difference that meets the eye is the grammatical one: *X wants to know* is normally followed by an indirect question (*whether* . . . , *what* . . . , *who* . . . , etc.); *X wants to believe*, however, normally requires the *that*-clause for an object. This second point is not surprising (we know that *believe* does not take *wh*'s); the first one is. Whereas it is perfectly normal to say that I do, or do not, want to believe that Joe is guilty, it is slightly odd to say that I do, or do not, want to know that Joe is guilty. It looks as if in the case of belief one were considering a particular proposition with a view of adopting it or not; one tries to choose, "make up one's mind," and in doing so one is motivated not only by reasons, but also by preference, prejudice, or caprice.[11] Indeed, the attitude of *I do not want to believe* . . . is like a struggle against a compulsive image. The posture of *I do not want to know* . . . , on the other hand, reminds one of closing one's eyes: one refuses to see what is there, or what might be there. Think of the accompanying gestures and words: *Don't tell me!* Correspondingly, wanting to know is like looking around (*whether* . . . , *what* . . . , *who* . . .) to see what is there.

[10] "Unde scis . . . ?" asked the Romans, and "Wovon wissen sie . . . ?" ask the Germans.
[11] Etymologically, *believe* is related to *love*, *know* to *can*.

Wanting to know is the sign of curiosity, wanting to believe is often the sign of credulity, and these two have nothing to do with one another.

Again, contrast the unbelievable with the unknowable. The unbelievable is something utterly unlikely, unexpected, or outrageous. The unknowable need not be any of these things; something may be quite simple and ordinary and yet unknowable, because we have no access to it. There is nothing unbelievable about Caesar's having had a birthmark on the small of his back, yet it is unknowable to us. Think of the parallel contrast between what cannot be imagined (that defies the imagination) and what cannot be seen. Knowledge, once more, is access to what is given; belief is the holding of an image, more or less freely chosen.

This is the reason why people can share beliefs but not "knowledges." The immediate object of believing is a belief, a picture of reality, and many persons can have the "same" belief, the "same" picture.[12] The immediate object of knowing, however, is not a "knowledge," a ("true") picture of reality, but reality itself.

X *knows that* p in most cases entails that X has learnt and has not forgotten that p. Now, is it forgetting that terminates beliefs? That X no longer believes that p does not indicate that he has forgotten that p. He might be aware of that proposition while disbelieving it; he just has changed his mind about it. Needless to say that no changing of one's mind turns knowledge into ignorance.

In view of all these arguments it is hard to see how the traditional account of knowledge in terms of belief could have enjoyed the favor of so many protagonists. This view, as far as

[12] In view of what we found in the previous chapter only "roughly" the same.

I can see, has no explanatory value at all. What, then, is its attraction?

It must be of the same nature as the lure of the phenomenalistic analysis of perception. As the sense-datum theory is an attempt to satisfy the skeptic about sense-perception, so the belief-theory is an attempt to appease the skeptic about knowledge. The questions, *How do you know that you really see when you think you see . . . ?* and *How do you know that you really know when you think you know . . . ?* are analogous. And the attempted answers, starting from the subjective, from sense-data and from beliefs, are also analogous.

Unfortunately, epistemology is one thing and conceptual analysis is another. Moreover, if the epistemologist wants to know what he is talking about, he should try to get his concepts clear before and not after answering the skeptic. Then, perhaps, the answers will turn out to be better.[13]

13 Concerning the matters mentioned in this last section, I greatly profited by some conversations with Professor Gilbert Ryle.

VI

Word and Concept

1. If a speaker (S) says something in a language (L) and one of the listeners (A) knows L but another (B) does not, then, normally, A will understand what S said but B will not. What is it, exactly, that A but not B succeeds in doing in this case, and how are we to account for the difference? It is obvious from what we have said thus far that no philosophy of language deserves that name without being able to provide an answer to this question. How great is then our disappointment when we realize that in our age, in which the philosophy of language is supposed to have come into its own, no satisfactory solution has yet been given to this problem of understanding.

There is, of course, a commonsense view, and, for want of anything clearly better, we may begin with that. It runs roughly as follows: B does not understand what S said because he does not know the meaning of the words that S used. Nor does he know, add the sophisticated, the structure of the sentence that

Word and Concept

S produced. A, on the other hand, knows what the words mean; moreover, knowing the structure as well, he is able to piece together the meaning of the sentence.

This, unfortunately, is not a very helpful answer. For, in the first place, it equates understanding a sentence, whatever that may be, with understanding what somebody said; moreover, the talk about piecing the meaning of the sentence together out of its ingredients is at best a vague metaphor, at worst sheer mythology; finally, it leaves the crucial concept of knowing the meaning of a word, let alone of a structure, unexplained.

Yet the commonsense view has at least one thing in its favor. It correctly assumes that the understanding of a unique complex, of what was said in a given speech-act, is to be explained in terms of understanding something more permanent and less complex (a sentence) and this in terms of knowing things still more abiding and simple (structures and words). For, as has been emphasized in contemporary writings, human beings are creative in their speech and there is a virtual infinity of things they can say. Even the number of sentences they may construe in doing so approaches infinity. The lexicon of any natural language contains a finite set of morphemes, however, and the syntax can presumably be reduced to an even smaller number of basic structures and recursive rules. Therefore, unless the task of understanding understanding is taken to be impossible, we have to assume that in each individual case the understanding of what is said is the result of a succession of moves, such as the identification of the illocutionary force, the recognition of the syntactic structure, and the processing of the semantic content. It would be naïve, of course, to imagine that these steps are as neatly distinct as this description might suggest. The tasks involved are in fact intertwined, but the general direction of the resolution must proceed from the complex to the simple, from the individual speech-act to the elementary structures and words involved.

This assumption does not contradict the claim I shall make later on that the very notion of a word is incomprehensible without the notion of a sentence, and that the concept of a sentence, in turn, is incomprehensible without the notion of a speech-act. Words and sentences are elements of a language, and a language is essentially an instrument for saying things. Thus I shall maintain, on the one hand, that the basic carriers of meaning are words; yet I shall also insist that words have meaning only because they can enter into sentences by means of which people can say something or other in many different ways. To use an old analogy again: understanding any particular chess position on the board depends upon our knowledge of the ways the pieces can move, yet the general concept of a piece or of a move depends upon the idea of what a chess game is.

2. Concerning the meaning of words, we may begin with the naïve view Wittgenstein attributes to St. Augustine in the first page of *Investigations*:

The individual words in language name objects—sentences are combinations of such names.—In this picture of language we find the roots of the following idea: Every word has a meaning. The meaning is correlated with the word. It is the object for which the word stands.[1]

---

[1] Part I, 1. It is quite clear, incidentally, that Wittgenstein severely misinterprets the Augustinian position; this "particular picture of the essence of human language" cannot be attributed to St. Augustine, not even on the basis of the passage quoted by Wittgenstein. It contains the following: "Their *intention* (my elders') was shown by their bodily movements, as it were *the natural language of all peoples* (verbis naturalibus omnium gentium): the expression of the face, the play of the eyes, the movement of

Word and Concept

I shall characterize this view by the slogan "meaning by association." Similar positions have been held by representatives of the empiricist tradition from Locke to Quine: the meaning of a word is given, typically, by its being associated with objects or mental images, with sense-data or concurrent stimuli, or with sets of these and similar things, according to the taste of the empiricist in question. It would amount to beating a dead horse, or a dying one at least, to try to refute this theory. Although I shall engage in such an exercise later on, for the time being I merely ask the reader to take the sentences in this essay one by one, or some sentences randomly chosen from any book, and see how such associations evoked by or attached to the individual words help him to understand what is being said. Even with the best will and the liveliest imagination, the hypothesis of meaning by association cannot be stretched to cover more than a fragment of our vocabulary, and the rest simply will not "take care of itself." [2]

This leaves another theory, more in vogue these days—the theory of "meaning by use." Again to speak roughly: the meaning of a word is given by its role in the language-game. In spite of the vagueness with which this view is usually expressed, I think it is far more promising than the first. But where does it leave us? In order to know what a word means, the speaker or

---

other parts of the body, and the tone of the voice *which expresses our state of mind* (. . . indicante affectionem animi) in seeking, having, rejecting, or avoiding something. Thus, as I heard words repeatedly used *in their proper places in various sentences*, I gradually learnt to understand what objects they signified; and . . . *I used them to express my own desires* (measque jam voluntates . . . per haec enuntiabam)" (*Confessions*, I.8, my italics). From the rest of this chapter it will appear that although I disagree with Wittgenstein's straw man, I agree with St. Augustine rather than with Wittgenstein.

[2] *Philosophical Investigations*, Part I, 1.

123

the listener must know how the game is played, that is, he must know the language. As Wittgenstein puts it in the *Blue Book*: "The sign (the sentence) gets its significance from the system of signs, from the language to which it belongs. Roughly: understanding a sentence means understanding a language." [3] If this is true of sentences, then it has to be true, *a fortiori*, of words. Reverting to our example: listener A knows the meaning of the words that S used because he knows L, whereas B does not know the meaning of those words because he does not know L. The happy result, then, is that A understands what S said in L because he knows L, and B fails to understand what S said in L because he does not know L. But this we have assumed at the beginning and have known all along.

3. If we ask what it is that would enable B to understand what S said, we suddenly realize that the above result is neither as happy nor as trivial as it at first appears. For, obviously, B must learn L to understand the speaker. Yet he cannot learn L word by word, because he will not know what any word in L means until he has mastered L, and he certainly cannot learn L "all at once." It seems to follow, therefore, that no one can learn a language at all. One may argue, of course, that B might know another language, say, L', so that he is able to replace elements in L' (words, structures, etc.) by the corresponding elements in L, and in this way, as it were, build a bridge step by step. The trouble is that the difficulty returns: how did he learn L', or whatever his first language might be? More generally, how do infants learn their mother tongue?

A similar problem arises, of course, with respect to the learning of such a game as chess. How can one learn the role of a piece without having an idea of the game "full blown"? Well,

[3] *The Blue and Brown Books*, p. 5.

for one thing, both the pupil and the teacher can talk; thus the teacher can explain the nature of the game. No such aid is available, however, in the learning of the first language. "But" —it may be objected—"often the pupil learns the game without any verbal instruction, merely by observing chess players." True —but not without arriving at the correct idea concerning the nature of the game. Obviously, he must be quite clever to be able to do this. And, I might add, he must be still more clever if he has had no previous acquaintance with any game. Then remember that a natural language, if viewed as a game, is an immensely complex one—consider just the syntax of German or Classic Greek and compare it with the rules of chess. Remember, too, that the typical learner of a first language is not a genius but a mere infant between two and four years of age. He need not be a *Wunderkind* either: *every* nonmoronic child is a fluent speaker of the language by the time he goes to school. Yet—unless he is a prodigy—he could not learn bridge, chess, or any other game of equal complexity.

Wittgenstein seems to suggest that the learning of a language is a matter of learning a number of specific language-games, such as asking, telling, and describing. This idea offers no solution, since the natural language is not the sum of, but the *system* of, all these "games": the same syntax, semantics, and phonetics run through them all, connect and govern them all. The implication of Wittgenstein's idea, therefore, is at best misleading in that it makes a difficult task look easy—it is like saying that chess is an easy game to learn, since all you have to know is how to push pawns, bishops, and the like around the board. Moreover, as I shall soon show, Wittgenstein's "games" cannot possibly capture the essence of speech at all.

St. Augustine, in his most explicit work on the subject, resorts to the inner teaching of God to explain this mystery,[4] and

4 *De Magistro*, Chs. XI–XIV.

rationalist thinkers, from Descartes to Chomsky, postulate a system of innate ideas. We are conditioned to smile at these suggestions, but as the alternatives vanish so may our smiles.

4. Since invoking the Holy Spirit, or admitting innate ideas, is a somewhat radical step, one has to be sure that it is impossible to learn a language word by word from scratch, that is without the possession of a previous language or of a structure more or less isomorphic with one.

A child, the empiricists tell us, does exactly that: equipped with only the most general learning strategies, he first learns what, say, *mama*, means, then what *bottle* means, then, after a while, what *rabbit* means, and so forth . . . till, somehow, he learns what such words as *unless, suspect,* and *deliberately* mean. One feels like adding: and then he lives happily ever after. In order to expose this fairy tale for what it is, let us look into the claim that it is possible for the infant to know what, for example, *bottle* means, in isolation. Well, when he sees a bottle he says "bottle," when he wants a bottle he says "bottle," and so forth. *Ergo* he knows what *bottle* means. Does he?

Suppose I condition a parrot to say "carrot" whenever I show him a banana and to peck at the banana on the fruit tray whenever I say "carrot." Moreover, let us assume for good measure that he also learns to say "carrot" whenever he wants a banana. A difficulty might arise here concerning the parrot's wanting a banana or, for that matter, the baby's wanting a bottle. What distinguishes these states in parrots or babies from wanting to eat, being hungry or thirsty, and the like, and willing to settle for the banana or the bottle (*full* bottle, by the way)? I shall brush this trouble aside. The important question is this: will the parrot know what the word *carrot* means? Of course he will not, for the word *carrot* does not mean . . . does not mean what?—a banana, this banana, this is a banana, is this a banana?, peck at the banana, I want a banana, . . . or what? You want to say that I should have conditioned the poor bird to say "banana" not "carrot" in those circumstances, and to peck at the banana at the word *banana* and not at the word *carrot*. Then he would use the word correctly. "Correctly" in what sense? Presumably in the sense of acting in agreement with the speakers of English. The trouble is that he would *not* be acting in agreement with those speakers. Do we say "banana" every time we see a banana or want one? Or do we touch the banana on the tray every time we hear that word? Drooling idiots apart, nobody behaves that way.

"Say what you like"—you may insist—"this is how children learn words . . . by associating bottles with *bottle*, bananas with *banana*, sitting down with *sitting down*, and so on." I agree, but we differ in the interpretation of the facts. These are indeed some of the ways in which the child gets to know what kind of thing is called a bottle or a banana, what sort of action is called sitting down. To be able to learn such things, however, he must come to understand what bottles and bananas are, what it is to sit down, and so forth; moreover, in order to know what these things are "called," he must have an idea of asserting and denying, describing and identifying, asking, giving, accepting, refusing, and so on. In other words, he must be able to fit these phrases into their place in a particular code which corresponds to a framework of thought he already possesses or progressively develops on his own.[5]

5. At this point the Wittgensteinian is likely to re-enter the fray and argue as follows. "No need for nebulous thought—at least not at this stage. For why should we not allow that the

[5] This, I think, is the sense of the Augustinian passage quoted by Wittgenstein (see n. 1).

word *carrot* 'means' *banana* in the little language game the parrot learned to play? Similarly, the child will first learn to use a very primitive language, consisting of a few nouns and permitting only a few moves. Later on he learns other moves and other words, until his language approximates ours, and his words begin to 'mean' things in the way ours normally do."

My reply is that no word learned in this way has any meaning in the parrot's language, simply because there is no such thing. Nor will the infant have any language so long as he merely responds to some words or produces them by way of a response. For there is no language without understanding, and merely responding to stimuli, vocal or otherwise, has little to do with understanding.

Wittgenstein asks us to imagine a language "consisting of the words 'block,' 'pillar,' 'slab,' 'beam.' A calls them out; B brings the stone which he has learnt to bring at such-and-such call. Conceive this as a complete primitive language." [6] ". . . Even the whole language of a tribe." [7] I have no trouble imagining creatures acting in this way. But I cannot conceive their behavior adding up to a language. Suppose A calls out to B (*to B*, say, by turning his face towards B) "slab." C, an on-looker, hears this. What is he to do? Are we to assume that everybody within earshot is supposed to grab the nearest slab? Were C to do such a thing it would show that he did not understand what A said. If, on the other hand, he does not do a thing, what does his understanding, if any, consist of? Shall we say, then, that he did not understand what A said? But he is supposed to know the language. . . .

I tell my dog, Fido, "sit!" Well trained as he is, he sits. One is inclined to say that he has understood and obeyed the order. Rover, within earshot, does not sit. What would it be for

6 *Philosophical Investigations*, Part I, 2.   7 *Ibid.*, 6

Word and Concept

Rover to understand the order? If I tell Johnny to sit down, Jimmy might understand what I said without doing anything. So can Johnny himself, of course, if he chooses to disobey. Not all orders are obeyed, but no order is obeyed or disobeyed without being understood. We blame the child for not obeying only if we know that he has understood the order. In more general terms, acting upon one's words presupposes the understanding of what has been said; consequently, understanding what has been said cannot be construed as acting upon one's words. Understanding is not acting, or reacting, one way or another, at all.

Commands, of course, load the dice: they call for action. Other speech-acts do not. I might say, "I think there is no life on Venus." How would you act upon my words? Some novels may bore you, may not move you at all. Yet your lack of reactions has nothing to do with the understanding of the text.

Wittgenstein's builder, A, pronounces the word "slab." B hears this, but does not bring the slab. This situation can be described in two ways. We might say that A merely provided a verbal stimulus, to which B had been trained to respond in a certain manner. If we put it this way, then all we can say about B is that, for some reason or another, he simply failed to respond. In this context the question of understanding does not arise at all. If, on the other hand, we claim that A said something rather than merely provided a stimulus, then we mean that he intended B to understand him—that is, intended him to realize that what A wanted him to do by saying "slab" was to bring the slab. But B can do this without bringing the slab. So can C, the passive witness, if he realizes what A intended to bring about *in B's mind* by uttering that word. Making the "game" more complex (by involving whole tribes and forms of life) does not help a bit to bridge the logical gap between responding to stimuli and understanding speech; the difference is not a matter of degree but of essence. The inherent aim of speech is not response but understanding; response may be *an* aim, but only through understanding. Incidentally, in a game, too, the players are supposed to understand what they are doing, not merely to respond. Even if I stop playing (say I catch the ball, but do not throw it back), I ought to know what I was supposed to do next. What Wittgenstein gives us is either an inadequate and misleading description of a game, or a description of something that is not even a game.

6. I suggested above that learning, for instance, what the word *bottle* means is equivalent to learning what kind of thing is called a bottle, which is impossible without learning what a bottle is (or, alternatively, what it is for something to be a bottle). Similarly with other "parts of speech": to know what the verb-phrase *sit down* means presupposes the knowledge of what it is to sit down, to know what *fat* means one has to know what it is to be fat, and to know what *deliberately* means one has to know what it is to do something deliberately.

Unfortunately, the light of this glaring piece of common sense has blinded most philosophers and semanticists alike, so that they have failed to see the obvious consequence: our knowledge of what a word means is a function of, and is to be explained in terms of, understanding certain incomplete propositions.

Consider, once more, the expressions we use in explaining what it is to know the meaning of words belonging to the various grammatical categories:

Nouns: what (*kind of thing*) *is a bottle*
            what it is (*for something*) *to be a bottle*

Word and Concept

Verbs: what it is *(for somebody or something) to sit down*

what it is *(for somebody or something) to push (something)*

Adjectives: what it is *(for somebody or something) to be fat*

Adverbs: what it is *(for somebody) (to do something) deliberately*

The propositional background of all but the first of the italicized expressions is obvious. Grammatically, they are nominalized sentences in which all slots but the one occupied by the word in question are filled by dummy words *(somebody, something, do)*. Thus we give the essential prerequisite of knowing the meaning of a word by stipulating a minimal environment ("kernel" frame). These frames, for the items other than the noun, are as follows:

N sits down
N pushes N
N is fat
N V (N) deliberately

The situation is not so clear with nouns; they do not have one, but many possible positions in kernel frames:

N V
N V N
N is N
N is A

Accordingly, whereas the phrase *(for something) to be a bottle* takes the noun in the third frame, the other, *a bottle is . . . (kind of thing)* takes it as a subject of possible "predicates" of various sorts. The fact that nouns, unlike the other classes, do

131

not have a definite kernel-type associated with them might account for the feeling of "saturation" with respect to substantive concepts versus the "unsaturated" impression given by concepts corresponding to verbs, adjectives, and (most of all) adverbs. With respect to these words we feel the pull toward the one specific pattern they connote. Nouns are pulled in many ways at the same time, so that the opposing forces cancel each other out; hence the impression of firmness in the concept.

7. In these last sentences I used the word *concept* intentionally. Knowing what a bottle is, what it is to sit down, and so on, is nothing but having a concept, or an idea, of these things. Indeed we speak of the concept of a bottle, or of the idea of doing something deliberately.[8] A concept, then, appears to be an open proposition, that is, a proposition in which some constituents are left undetermined. Accordingly, as the linguistic expression of a proposition is a sentence, so the linguistic expression of a concept is a sentence frame partly filled by dummy words.

Obviously, some concepts are more complex than others: think of the idea of potatoes, planting potatoes, planting potatoes in a backyard, and so forth. As the sentences fill up (need fewer dummies), the concepts become more and more complex. Yet, in spite of the obvious correlation between concepts and their verbal expression, we must not conclude that there is a complete isomorphism between verbal and conceptual structures. As the "generative semanticists" have recently shown, one word (e.g., *remind*) may cover a complex structure of ideas.[9] And, as I show in Appendix II, a simple root like *break*

[8] The word *idea* is particularly suited to incomplete propositions; e.g.: *I have an idea what he did* or . . . *where he is*, etc.

[9] See the Bibliography under Fillmore, Lakoff, McCawley, and Postal.

Word and Concept

seems to code a more complex idea than its derivative *broken*. Often a conceptual structure which has a one-word encoding in one language requires many words in others; think of our old friend, the "inquisitive" *wonder*, which has no one-word equivalent in French or German, or of *igloo*, which requires at least two (*snow-house?*) in domestic English.

And speaking of *snow-house*, what about *dog-house?* The former is *made of* snow, the latter is *made for* dogs. Similarly, whereas a snowman is *made of* snow, an iceman *sells* ice. These examples show clearly that perfectly analogous verbal constructs may be used to encode quite dissimilar conceptual structures. Transformationalists will object that the deep structure of these phrases is different. Granted, but what is this deep structure? It is not something pronounced in speech, or spelled out in writing; it is something understood by the speaker and the hearer. Of course, in trying to *exhibit* the deep structure, words turn up again, but not alone: one uses "trees," category symbols, and the like. The deep structure of a sentence, as given, say, in a Chomsky-tree, is the result of an attempt—a very laudable attempt—to stretch the code to display all details of the message. It is a step toward the rationalistic ideal of a "perfect" language, a language isomorphic with the structure of thought. The next step—less laudable—is to assume that in fact we think in such a language, in "mentalese" as some would call it. This cannot be, of course, because there is no language that cannot be spoken; and nobody can speak (openly or in one's imagination) mentalese. What is true is that we think in concepts and, as we will see, the formation of our concepts is influenced by the language(s) we speak.

Consider the sentence, *I saw her duck when the stone fell, and then it swam away.*[10] What causes the mental gasp when

[10] This sentence I heard attributed to Thomas A. Patton.

133

it swam comes along? The necessity to reinterpret what went before. How do we do this? By mentally rattling off paraphrases? Or by seeing tree-structures grow in the imagination? Not at all—yet we understand all right.

8. The "dummies" used in the phrases expressing a concept are not quite blank: not every word of the appropriate grammatical category can fit into the slots marked by the dummies. Compare, for example, the concepts of pushing and believing. The subject slot in the linguistic expression of the former admits most of what may be called physical-object nouns (yet certain mobility is presupposed), but the corresponding slot in the expression of the latter concept admits only human nouns. The object slot of *believe*, moreover, requires very special filling, namely, nominalized sentences, whereas the object domain of *push* comprises practically the same set of nouns as its subject range. Now, if we may coin a slogan, the context shows the concept. Accordingly, the dictionary definition of a word, which either summarizes its syntactical constraints and cooccurrence restriction by means of such syntactic and semantic "markers" as *transitive verb, animate,* and *human,* or displays them in typical contexts, is a mighty aid in the mastering of a concept, and, *faute de mieux,* is often taken for the definition of the concept itself. In most cases, needless to say, the features thus far mentioned will not define a single, unique concept but a group of closely related ones. Think of the concepts of colors, metals, and animals of the same family, or, to stay closer to home, such speech-acts as stating, asserting, and alleging. Further distinguishing marks or presuppositions will be needed to round out the definition.[11]

There are certain words for which the account just given does

11 For further details on lexicography, see, e.g., J. J. Katz, *The Philosophy of Language.*

not work. Prepositions, articles, quantifiers, pronouns, auxiliaries, connectives, and the like do not connote any specific kernel frame, nor do they suggest specific cooccurrence restrictions. Consequently, except in a somewhat forced philosophical context, we do not speak of knowing the concept, or having the idea, of *the, but, which,* or *shall.* Think of the notorious "philosophical" difficulties besetting the notions of *being, sameness,* and *doing.* Such words are but grammatical constants or linguistic dummies; consequently their "concept" will amount to a mere empty frame. With prepositions we try heroically; we try to understand what it is for something to be *between* something and something else, or even what it is for something to be *with* or *by* something else.

By and large, however, to know the meaning of a word is to be able to assign it to a concept, that is, to be aware of the range of minimal propositions that can be expressed by using that word. Meaning is not a word-and-object nexus; it is a word-and-concept relation.

9. "But surely"—it may be objected—"knowing the meaning of a word enables one to describe, pick out, or produce objects belonging to the kind the word denotes. If you know what the word *dog* means, you will be able to identify dogs for other people, if you know what *pink* means you will be able to pick out the pink flowers in the vase when asked for, and if you know what *triangle* means you will be able to draw one if requested." I agree to this extent: in many cases, knowing what a certain kind of thing is called enables me to do such things, in much the same way as knowing where I live enables me to walk home. Yet, if I am paralyzed, shackled, or blinded, or if it is pitch-dark outside, or if I happen to be in Timbuktu, I will not be able to walk home. Such an inability, however, will not diminish one whit my knowledge of where I live. Similarly,

although I could not possibly pick out molybdenum from a sample of rare metals, or tell a chiliagon from a 1001-sided polygon, my knowledge of what these things are, and, consequently, of what these words mean, is not at all impaired by this inability. Only the chicken sexer can tell a male chick from a female chick; yet we all know, no less than the chicken sexer, what chicks are and what the difference is between the male and the female. The chicken sexer's extra "sense" which enables him to do his job has nothing in common with the "sense" for fine shades of meaning. Finally, it would be insane to suggest that the blind John Milton had lost some of his knowledge of English, or that Helen Keller did not know the meaning of most of our common words.

Another, somewhat more sophisticated attempt to tie meaning to the world may be made along the following lines. We have come to the conclusion that the concept, which gives the meaning of a word, is nothing but an open proposition; in other words, to know what a word means is to be aware of its propositional potential. Propositions, however, the logic texts tell us, are the things that are true or false. Consequently, our knowledge of what a word means necessarily points to the state of affairs that would make propositions true. Hence the various "alethic" theories of meaning, with their myopic concern with truth, verification, and verifiability as the only dimension in which propositions can be viewed and assessed.

Yet, as we know by this time, one can say things in many different ways, with this or that "illocutionary force" specified, or at least specifiable, by the use of a performative verb. In the same way, as we have also seen, propositions can also be entertained or arrived at in thought in more than one way. Now the issue of truth and falsity arises only in connection with certain illocutions, such as stating, asserting, admitting, and testifying, and only with certain mental acts or states, such as believing, guessing, or suspecting. Other acts of speech and thought hardly raise this issue at all. Think of orders, proposals, resolutions, and resignations on the one hand, and decisions, wishes, and intentions on the other. Orders are easy or difficult, proposals feasible or unfeasible, decisions wise or foolish, intentions noble or base, and so on. I do not say that these are the only respects in which these acts can be assessed; nor, however, is the aspect of truth the only one appropriate to statements, beliefs, and the like. Statements, in addition to being true or false, can be assessed as being inappropriate, irrelevant, superficial, or the contraries of these. Similarly, beliefs may be praised for being well founded or blamed for being unreasonable, quite apart from their being true or false. Nevertheless, with these things, unlike the previous ones, the issue of truth is a relevant, nay a centrally important, consideration.

Compare the utterances:

> I order you to occupy the city
> I forbid you to occupy the city
> I expect that you will occupy the city.

If the conditions spelled out in Chapter IV are satisfied, then one can say that here the same thing, your occupation of the city, is ordered, forbidden, or claimed to be expected. Similarly, the next day, your occupation of the city may be reported or denied, approved of or regretted. In all these cases the same proposition, your occupying the city, is viewed in several dimensions, such as desirability, feasibility, likelihood, truth, and so forth. Thus it is not the proposition as such that is, say, true or feasible, but the proposition as entertained in a certain mental frame or issued with a certain illocutionary force. The sentence *The cat is on the mat* is not true or false, nor is the proposition that the cat is on the mat; what is true or false is someone's *assertion* that the cat is on the mat. Provided, of course, that an assertion has indeed been made and not merely an attempt at making one, vitiated by some infelicity such as the lack of a suitable cat. Similarly, the sentence *I shall pay you $1000.00 tomorrow*, or the proposition that I shall do so, is in no way irresponsible, but my promise to that effect, provided that I succeeded in making one, might be irresponsible.

I have implied above that occupying a city is occupying a city, whether it is ordered or reported, suggested or forbidden, in the same way as a cat is a cat, whether it sleeps or eats, whether it is kicked or cuddled. Yet, obviously, it belongs to the understanding of what a cat is that it can eat or can be kicked. So too, it belongs to the understanding of the proposition that one occupies the city that it can be ordered or that it can be true. Mathematical propositions, for instance, cannot be ordered or regretted. They can be deduced from axioms, however, which can hardly be said of that proposition about the city. The sole dimension of truth and falsity cannot determine the understanding of a proposition, although the existence of this perspective does contribute to the understanding of most propositions.

Knowing the meaning of a word is having the ability to assign it to a concept, that is, being aware of the range of minimal propositions that can be expressed by using that word. This, in turn, requires the comprehension of speech-acts and mental states appropriate to the propositions in question. This result, of course, is nothing but a reformulation of Wittgenstein's insight that knowing what a word means presupposes the mastery of a language, or something closely isomorphic with a language, "full-blown."

138

Word and Concept

10. If this is so, the problem that haunted us at the beginning returns with undiminished force: how is it possible to learn a language at all?

To begin with, there is no great problem about learning a second language. If I am told that the German verb *glauben* means the same as the English *believe*, then I know to what concept this word is to be assigned. I may have to correct some hasty assumptions later on, if I discover a divergence in the conceptual structures embedded in the two languages. I will learn, for instance, that there are two verbs in German, *kennen* and *wissen*, that divide the burden carried by the English verb *know*. Such adjustments, however, will remain accidental, for, as far as we know, all languages are intertranslatable; consequently each particular language must have the latitude and built-in flexibility to accommodate the idiosyncrasies of other languages. What seems to be impossible is to learn a language which is *not* intertranslatable with our own. And this conclusion is not at all strange.

What, then, about the learning of the first language? How is that to be explained? Children appear to learn their mother tongue not in one step but in many, almost word by word. Yet we have found that the learning of a word, as a meaningful element, not only presupposes the existence of a framework of thought, but also the ability to understand and to perform a variety of speech-acts, which, in turn, requires some command over the very complex system the syntactic and semantic structure of a natural language represents. Since there is no evidence of learning by osmosis, or of an infusion of knowledge by the Holy Ghost or similar agency, and since the idea that every nonmoronic infant is so clever as to divine the real nature of this immensely complex "game" without any previous acquaintance with any game (and without the simultaneous ability to learn any other game of any complexity) is clearly absurd, the most reasonable explanation is that a child must learn his native tongue in a way similar to the way one learns a second language. He must have, in other words, a native equipment that codes the fundamental illocutionary, syntactic, and semantic features of any possible human language. It is not my intention to claim that this apparatus is present in the infant at birth; therefore, I shall not call it innate. It is native, however, in the sense that its development is spontaneous and genetically determined in such a way that, according to the best evidence, it enables a child, between the ages of one and a half and four years, to come to understand and to display all the basic linguistic moves.[12]

Such a system of native "ideas" provides the framework which is then filled up progressively through the influence of a more specific code representing the features of the mother tongue. It makes sense, therefore, to speak of one basic conceptual framework, which is the matrix underlying the various natural languages. It is, to paraphrase Leibniz, like a preliminary sketch for a painting, or rather a mosaic, which specifies the structure yet leaves the colors and fine details undetermined. Learning a word, for the child, is like fitting a stone into the appropriate place in the mosaic.

11. As for the content of this native stock of concepts, we can at the present time do no more than make educated guesses. Yet, I think, the task of spelling it out in detail is not an im-

---

[12] Beards are native to human males but, fortunately, not innate.

For recent empirical evidence supporting the theory developed here, see the bibliography under Lennenberg and under Smith and Miller.

Word and Concept

possible one: Aristotle, Descartes, Kant, and recently Chomsky have succeeded in marking out some domains that must belong to this framework. We have found, ourselves, that the native conceptual structure must contain semantic, syntactic, and illocutionary factors (see Appendix III).

These are, then, the "clear and distinct" ideas which lend intelligibility to the rest. They are "a priori" in origin and self-contained in their development: experience cannot change their content. No experience is relevant to one's idea of what it is to assert or to request something; what it is to believe or to decide; what is truth or necessity; what is a person, an object, a process, or a state; what are change, purpose, causation, time, extension, and number. If these ideas need clarification, the way to obtain it is to reflect on what we all implicitly know and show forth in the correct use of language, and, in certain domains, to offer models or formalizations to aid and further develop our understanding.

This is not the case with "empirical" ideas; they remain open to experience. Do we really know what a dog is? Or did we really know, before modern physics, the difference between yellow and blue? What we cannot tell we show and illustrate (think of pictures in the dictionary); what we cannot understand we represent in the imagination and hope to learn more about from experience. Moreover, we do not rest until we are able to define these things in exact, mainly mathematical, terms, which, presumably, rest on clear and distinct ideas. This has happened in physics and chemistry and is happening in biology. We feel that we best understand nature, the realm of the empirical, in mathematical terms.

Notice, incidentally, that the element of subjectivity affecting certain propositions does not carry over into the domain of concepts. Reference does not enter into the open propositions that amount to the concepts, and the corresponding linguistic expressions, the "kernel frames" as we called them, are devoid of the referential apparatus of the language (names, demonstrative pronouns, the definite article, etc.). Even the "images" just mentioned in connection with certain empirical ideas are of the "abstract" type described in section 11 of Chapter IV. In any case, with or without a "phantasm," all concepts are universal, and, as a consequence, essentially intersubjective.

To sum up, the development of one's conceptual repertory is the result of three factors: the unfolding native equipment, the exposure to experience, and the "feedback" effect of learning this or that particular language. For learning a specific language—whether first, second, or third—is learning a code in which to express one's thoughts and to recover the thoughts expressed by others. The use of any code, however, will affect to some extent the message itself, and ultimately the very organization of one's own thoughts and their organic encoding, whatever that may be, in one's nervous system. An analogy may help here. As the same word can be encoded in spoken or written symbols, the same concept, and the same thought, can be encoded in the various languages *and* in the "code," as yet unknown, operating in the human nervous system. The agent, of course, is not aware of the operation of this latter "code" in the way in which he is aware of the former. Yet, as far as I can see, the deciphering of the organic encoding of human thought remains a scientific possibility.

Thus when speaker *S* says something in language *L*, *A*, who knows *L*, will understand what *S* said, because he is able to decode the message and identify the content in the familiar world of his own thoughts. This is a task that proceeds on many levels: recognition of the illocutionary force, determination of reference, and establishment of the semantic reading of the sentence from the structure and the words.[13] I cannot discuss here the details of this very complex affair, but merely point out that owing to the finite repertory of elements involved on each of these levels there is no mystery about our ability to understand the potentially infinite number of things people might say in their various speech-acts.

In spite of the feedback effect just mentioned, one's own thoughts are not in any specific language. As there are no Roman or Arabic numbers, though there are Roman and Arabic numerals, so there are no English thoughts and German concepts, although thoughts and ideas can be expressed in English or German, some of them with greater ease and facility in the one language than in the other. Thus we are not forced to deny the possibility of thoughts in intelligent deaf-mutes, or the good sense of saying, "I do not find the exact word for what I want to say." Finally, to ask a bilingual person, in all generality, "In what language do you think?" is to ask a silly question. One might as well ask whether he thinks in speech, writing, or pantomime.

[13] This last level seems to be fairly independent of the previous two: it corresponds to the notion of understanding a sentence as distinct from understanding what one said by using that sentence in a given speech act.

VII

Descartes' Res Cogitans

Thinking

1. If I am accused at this point of holding an essentially Cartesian view of ideas, thought, and speech, and, in general, of the human mind, then I must plead guilty to the charge. I do not *feel* guilty though, since, if Professor Ryle is right—and he is in this matter—this puts me in the good company of those who profess the "prevalent theory," the "official doctrine." [1] He attributes the prevalence of this doctrine to the enormous influence of Descartes. Here I differ with him, and claim that the "official doctrine" is nothing but the commonsense view, and is Cartesian only inasmuch as it has found its clearest philosophical expression in Descartes' works.

Presently I shall review the main points of Descartes' psychology and compare them with our results. I shall not do this in order to bolster my theory with his authority. The process of justification will go the other way: I intend to show that our

[1] *The Concept of Mind*, p. 11.

144

conclusions vindicate the substance of his doctrine. Having cast away the fixed ideas and prejudices fostered upon us by an empiricist past and a behaviorist present, we are going to realize that the main lines of his position are sound and correct. As may be expected, we will also discover the traces of other prejudices, religious and philosophical, in Descartes himself, causing him to say things he should not have said had he remained faithful to his own principles throughout. By assessing the Cartesian doctrine in the light of our own findings, and by correcting his mistakes, I hope to project an outline of an integrated philosophical view of man as a thinking thing, a sketch of "rational" psychology—certainly not official, not even complete, but true as far as it goes.

This procedure will yield another advantage: in reviewing the Cartesian position we will encounter certain topics which, though germane to our concern, have not been given adequate consideration in the previous chapters, mainly because of my particular point of departure. Whereas I have talked a great deal about speech, thought, knowledge, and ideas, the notion of sensation has hardly been taken up despite its obvious relation to the concept of thought. Again, although I have laid the foundations for a doctrine of the self, it is obviously desirable to say more and to be more explicit about it. Fortunately Descartes helps us to remedy both deficiencies: concerning sensation, because he was so wrong; concerning the self, because he came so tantalizingly close to the truth. Accordingly, in the following discussion I shall pursue these two topics in somewhat greater detail than the others. There remains another large omission in my treatment of the "thinking thing," and here Descartes does not help us. I mean the problems of action and choice, which are obviously tied up with intention, decision, and other forms of thought. These topics, however, important and involved as they are, would require another work of comparable length.

In surveying the main points of the Cartesian theory I shall speak to the reader who is fairly familiar with at least the better known parts of the Cartesian opus. Thus I shall not attempt to support obvious claims by detailed references to the texts. On more controversial points, however, I shall let Descartes speak for himself, often in longer quotations, and often from lesser known works. Where the translation might be misleading, I shall insert the original phrases.[2]

2.   The cornerstone of Descartes' psychology is the notion of thought. "What then am I? A thing which thinks. What is a thing which thinks? It is a thing which doubts, understands, (conceives), affirms, denies, wills, refuses, which also imagines and feels."[3] Here, at the focal point of his most important work, Descartes spells out what he means by *thinking* (*cogitare, penser*). The list he gives is highly condensed, and follows a classificatory scheme that betrays the author's scholastic training. Although he begins—*à propos* of the topics previously discussed—with a more specific item, namely doubt, the sequel neatly corresponds to the standard scholastic headings. First *apprehensio simplex* (i.e., understanding and conception), then *iudicium* (i.e., "mental" affirmation and denial[4]), then *appetitus intellectualis* (i.e., will and refusal), and finally the

[2] For the original texts I shall use the Adam-Tannery edition (indicated by AT). Whenever possible, I quote from the Haldane-Ross translation (HR). If not credited, the translation is mine. In the translations, I have often added words and phrases in brackets; words and phrases in parentheses were supplied by Haldane and Ross.

[3] *Meditation II*: AT VII, 28; HR I, 153.

[4] ". . . To affirm to oneself that . . . , an act that needs no language [quod fit sine voce]." *Replies III*: AT VII, 182–183; HR II, 69.

"mixed" operations of imagination and feeling. In some corresponding passages the traditional classification is taken over undiluted: "understanding, willing, imagining, feeling, etc.";[5] "willing, understanding, imagining, feeling, etc."[6] In the *Principles* he explicitly attributes all the "modes" of thinking to two "general modes," operation of the intellect and operation of the will.[7]

Thus the list given in *Meditation II* is not intended to be a detailed or exclusive enumeration of the modes of thought. Indeed, only a few lines later Descartes claims that he is the being "who desires to know more, is averse from being deceived,"[8] and at the beginning of *Meditation III* he adds, "that knows a few things, . . . (that loves, that hates),"[9] and so forth.

Moreover, since at this stage of the *Meditations* he has discarded all beliefs in the existence of anything other than himself ("thus holding converse only with myself"[10]), any move he makes in the course of his reflections must belong to that thinking thing, must be an instance of a certain mode of thought. Thus it is he, *qua* thinking thing, that considers, examines, and investigates certain matters and inquires into them; that understands and comprehends some ideas; that believes, recollects (recalls to memory), or assumes certain propositions; that sees, finds out, recognizes, and discovers their truth or falsity; that derives and concludes things and tries to convince himself of their truth; that judges issues and distinguishes ideas and attributes them to one source or another. It is he, the thinking thing, to whom things occur and who pays attention to them

---

[5] *Reply III*: AT VII, 176; HR II, 64.
[6] Letter (to Mersenne), Apr. 1637: AT I, 366.
[7] I, XXXII: AT VIII, 17; HR I, 232.   [8] AT VII, 28; HR I, 153.
[9] AT VII, 34; HR I, 157.
[10] *Meditation III*: AT VII, 34; HR I, 157.

and gives them the right to occupy his mind; who is often amazed and astonished at what he finds; who aspires perfection, hopes for certainty, and tries to avoid error. Finally he is the one who sees, who hears, who feels, and who feigns things in his imagination. And do not forget that he, the thinking thing, "holds converse with himself," "interrogates" himself, "affirms," "denies," and "says" many things, "remarks" upon certain matters, and "complains" about others.

Enough said. It is obvious that, with the notable exception of imagination and sensation, the Cartesian concept of thought and thinking is identical with the one developed in Chapter III above. One could, in fact, collect a significant portion of the "thinking" verbs, in each category, from the text of the *Meditations* alone. And the whole of the *Meditations* is nothing but a record of his "thinking about" a variety of problems, an orderly process of moving from thought to thought. Notice, in particular, the presence of the performative verbs mentioned at the end of the previous paragraph among Descartes' own verbs of thought. This reminds us of Austin's tendency to list verbs of thought among verbs of saying. Both authors are victims of the "leakage" between these two genera pointed out earlier in our discussion. Descartes, at any rate, is conscious of the parallelism between thinking and saying: remember the formulation of the *Cogito* argument in *Meditation II:* "This proposition: I am, I exist, is necessarily true each time that I *pronounce* it, or that I *mentally* conceive it [quoties a me profertur, vel mente concipitur]" [11]. The same proposition: a common object of speech and thought. Later on I shall return to this point.

Incidentally, even the traditional division of purely mental operations into those of the intellect and those of the will is

[11] AT VII, 25; HR II, 150 (my italics).

not entirely alien to our own classification. Clearly, the apprehensives, putatives, recognitives, and assessives are verbs denoting "intellectual" (or "cognitive") acts and states, whereas the resolutives and conatives belong to the "voluntary" domain. The traditional division of the mental faculties into intellect and will can be viewed as a somewhat rough, intuitive approximation of this fact.[12]

Sensation

3. As for imagination and sensation, we seem to differ. Descartes consistently maintains that feelings, and sensations, as well as the products of one's fancy, are one and all modes of thought. Insisting upon the propositional nature of all thought, I did not regard these things as thoughts. Common sense, as we have seen, supports the view that sensations of light, of sound, of hunger, and so forth, are not part of one's thinking, nor is the spontaneous flight of the imagination one might experience in daydreams or real dreams, or while thinking about unrelated matters.[13] Some sensations, notably aches, pains, pangs of hunger, blinding light, and strong noise, are not only not counted among our thoughts, but they are apt to interfere with our thinking, and, in extreme cases, may stop it al-

[12] Descartes himself, owing to his peculiar brand of "voluntarism" (developed in *Meditation IV*) cuts the cake along different lines: "Thus sense-perception, imagination, and conceiving things that are purely intelligible, are just different methods of perceiving; but desiring, holding an aversion, affirming, denying, doubting, all these are the different modes of willing" (*Principles*, I, XXXII: AT VIII, 17; HR I, 232).

[13] E. Anscombe and P. T. Geach suggest, in their Translators' Note to *Descartes' Philosophical Writings* (pp. XLVIIf), that the word *pensée* (and *cogitatio*) might have been used more tolerantly in Descartes' age. I do not think, however, that his position was due to any such latitude of usage; as we are going to see, he had definite philosophical reasons for regarding sensations as thoughts.

together. In a similar way, it will be recalled, the lascivious and unwelcome play of St. Antony's imagination did not embellish his meditations on the holy mysteries; he had to overcome or ignore it in order to pursue the train of his thought. We must not forget, of course, what we were forced to realize in Chapter IV: in thinking about individuals, and in certain other thoughts as well, perception and imagination re-enter the domain of thought, but only inasmuch as they form an ingredient in some mental act or other.

On the other hand, not even Descartes regards feeling and imagination on a par with the "pure" forms of thought. In listing these modes he usually appends the former by a phrase indicating a gap: "What is a thing which thinks? It is a thing which doubts, understands, (conceives), affirms, denies, wills, refuses, which *also* imagines and feels [imaginans quoque et sentiens]." [14] "Taking the word thought [pensée], as I do, for all the operations of the soul . . . not only the meditations and the volitions, but *even* [mais mesme] the functions of sight, hearing, . . . etc." [15]

There are, of course, more explicit texts to the same point: "I remark besides that this power of imagination which is in one, inasmuch as it differs from the power of understanding, is in no wise a necessary element in my nature or in (my essence, that is to say, in) the essence of my mind: for although I did not possess it I should doubtless ever remain the same as I now am." [16] Later on, in the same Meditation, he speaks of "the faculties of imagination and feeling, without which I can easily conceive myself clearly and distinctly as a complete

[14] *Meditation II:* AT VII, 28; HR I, 153 (my italics).
[15] Letter, March 1638: AT II, 36 (my italics).
[16] *Meditation VI:* AT VII, 73; HR I, 186.

being." [17] To P. (Gibieuf) he writes: "Imagination . . . sensation . . . belong to the soul, because they are kinds of thought
[espèces de pensées]; nevertheless they belong to the soul only
insofar as it is joined to the body, and for this reason they are
the kinds of thought without which one can conceive the soul
absolutely pure." [18]

4. Sensation and imagination are to him "mixed" modes, per-
taining to both the body and the soul. Since only the soul can
think, only a part of these things can be called thought. Which
part? In his *Reply to Objections* VI he distinguishes three
grades (gradus) of sensation. "To the first belongs the immediate affection of the bodily organ by external objects." [19]
This level of sensation is purely mechanical, common to all
animals, and is not thinking, not even to Descartes. "The
second comprises the immediate mental result . . . ; such are
the perceptions [perceptiones] of pain, of pleasurable stimula-
tion, of thirst, of hunger, of colours, of sound, savour, odour,
cold, heat, and the like." [20] These "raw" sensations count for
thought with Descartes but not with us. "Finally the third
contains all those judgements [iudicia] which, on the occasion
of motions occurring in the corporeal organ, we have from our
earliest years been accustomed to pass about things external
to us." [21] This level is thinking both to him and to us. Similar
distinctions might be drawn with respect to the imagination,
since "all the same things which the soul perceives by the intermission of the nerves, may also be represented by the fortuitous
course of the animal spirits, without there being any other dif-

[17] *Ibid:* AT VII, 78; HR I, 190.
[18] Letter (to P. [Gibieuf]), Jan. 1642: AT III, 478.
[19] *Reply* VI: AT VII, 436–37; HR II, 251.   [20] *Ibid.*   [21] *Ibid.*

ference excepting that the impressions which come into the
brain by the nerves are usually more lively or definite than those
excited there by the spirits. . . . The former resemble the
shadow or the picture of the latter." [22]

Having thus pinned down the point of our disagreement on
the second level of sensation (and imagination), the question
arises as to the significance of this difference: is it a mere ter-
minological disagreement, or does it involve matters of substance?

I have no doubt that the latter is the case. For, to begin with,
this "extended" conception of thought directly leads Descartes
to the notorious doctrine of the automatism of brutes, perhaps
the most counterintuitive item in his philosophy. Moreover, as
our discussion of this particular problem will show, Descartes'
view involves him in a persistent equivocation concerning the
notion of thinking: whereas he explicitly maintains that sensation and imagination are forms of thinking, in his arguments
that turn upon this concept he implicitly seems to operate with
the "restricted" notion, that is, with the idea of thought that
I have developed. The reasons for this curious ambivalence will
open an interesting perspective on the very essence of the
Cartesian revolution.

5. How does he show that animals cannot think? The most
explicit text is from the famous letter to Henry More:

But the principal argument, to my mind, which may convince us
that the brutes are devoid of reason [bestias cogitatione destitutas
esse] is that . . . although all of them make us clearly understand
their natural movement [impetus naturales] of anger, of fear, of
hunger, and others of like kind, either by the voice or by other
bodily motions, it has never yet been observed that any animal has

[22] *The Passions of the Soul*, I, 26: AT XI, 348; HR I, 343.

Descartes' Res Cogitans

arrived at such a degree of perfection as to make use of a true language [vera loquela]; that is to say, as to be able to indicate to us
by the voice, or by other signs, anything which could be referred
to thought alone, rather than to a movement of mere nature [ad
solam cogitationem, non autem ad impetum naturalem]; for the
word [loquela] is the sole sign and the only certain mark of the
presence of thought hidden and wrapped up in the body; now all
men, the most stupid and the most foolish, those even who are deprived of the organs of speech, make use of signs, whereas the
brutes never do anything of the kind; which may be taken for the
true distinction [vera differentia] between man and brute.[23]

An earlier letter is even more explicit on what animals can and
cannot do: "It cannot be said that they talk among themselves
but we do not understand them; for, as dogs and other animals
express to us their passions [leurs passions], they would express
to us as well their thoughts [pensées], if they had them," [24]
much the same way as "the deaf and dumb invent particular
signs by which they express their thoughts." [25]

We may recapitulate the argument as follows. Animals do
not talk, that is, do not express thoughts. They do express,
however, their passions. Now, if they had thoughts as well, they
would express them or at least try to express them. Therefore,
they have no thoughts. What are these passions (or *impetus
naturales*) that they do express? Descartes obliges us with some
examples: anger, fear, hunger, and the like;[26] joy and pain and
the like.[27] That is to say, passions in the "most general signifi-

[23] Letter (to Morus), Feb. 1649: AT V, 278; *Descartes Selections* (ed.
R. M. Eaton), p. 360.
[24] Letter (to the Marquis of Newcastle), Nov. 1646: AT IV, 575;
Eaton, p. 357.
[25] *Ibid.*
[26] Letter (to Morus), Feb. 1649: AT V, 278; Eaton, p. 360.
[27] Letter (to the Marquis of Newcastle), Nov. 1646: AT IV, 574;
Eaton, p. 356.

153

cance" of this word, which include sensation, feeling, and imagination.[28] If the argument is to have any force, Descartes must assume that what the beasts express is nothing more than sensation on the first level mentioned above. For, if it is sensation on the second level, then it is thought; consequently, the cry or the whimper of a hungry, scared, or wounded animal would have to qualify as an expression of thought.

As far as I can see, nothing entitles Descartes to make this assumption. In humans, the typical pre-verbal manifestations—cries, gestures, postures, faces, and so forth—that can be described as spontaneous expressions of fear, hunger, and pain, are the expressions of sensations actually experienced by the subject, not merely terminal stages of a physiological chain of events. It would not even make sense to talk of these manifestations as "expressing" anything, if this latter were the case. Why, then, should it be otherwise in the case of the brutes?

Descartes cannot have it both ways. If he argues from the fact that animals do express feelings like us, but do not express thoughts as we do, then he cannot maintain, at the same time, that what animals do express—sensations, passions, et cetera—are not at all like our sensations and passions. Thus, whereas he succeeds in showing that animals do not think in the sense of "thinking" developed earlier in this book, he fails to show that they do not think in his own sense of "thinking." What he demonstrates is that animals have no thoughts—that is, that they do not perform mental operations the objects of which can be expressed in speech. He fails to prove, however, that animals do not have real sensations and feelings, emotions and passions—that is, experiences the spontaneous expression of which is not an act of speech, but a whimper, a cry, a grimace,

28 *Passions*, I, 25: AT XI, 348; HR I, 343.

or a posture. For, in exhibiting these manifestations, the animal, or the man, does not perform a speech-act, does not say anything.

6. Descartes had but one criterion for recognizing thoughts: consciousness or immediate awareness. "By the name thought I understand all things that occur in us in such a way that we are conscious of them, inasmuch as we are conscious of them [Latin: . . . quae nobis consciis in nobis fiunt, quantenus eorum in nobis conscientia est]"; [29] ". . . in such a way that we are immediately aware of them by ourselves [French: . . . de telle sorte que nous l'appercevons immediatement par nous-mesmes]." [30] Given this criterion, it is not surprising that he regards sensations as thoughts. In a sense (but only in a sense, as I shall point out later on), these things are as immediately "given" to us as, say, our insights, beliefs, intentions, and decisions. It makes no more sense to ask somebody how he knows that he is in pain than it does to ask him how he knows that he wants to go to Paris, or that he just decided to go by airplane.

Our concept of thought is restricted to a part of this domain, namely to mental acts, states, and processes with propositional content. Descartes, as far as I can see, never succeeded in catching this distinction, and to him sensation remained a sort of "confused" thinking. In other words, instead of the specific distinction between the propositional and the nonpropositional, all he sees is a difference of degree between the clear and the confused. It is understandable, therefore, that although he insists upon the conceivability of the human mind "toute pure,"

[29] *The Principles of Philosophy*, I, 9: AT VIII, 7.
[30] AT IX–2, 28.

without sensations, passions, and imagination, he claims that these modes "cannot be so conceived without me, that is without an intelligent substance in which they reside, for (. . .) in their formal concept, some kind of intellection [intellectionem nonnullam] is comprised.[31]

In the following passage he explicitly confuses feeling and the internal judgment consequent upon feeling: "If one wants to conclude to one's existence from the sentiment or the opinion [du sentiment ou de l'opinion] that one breathes . . . one concludes very well; because this thought [cette pensée] of breathing appears to our mind before the thought of our existence, and because we cannot doubt that we have it [que nous ne l'ayons], when we have it." [32]

Yet it is obvious that the feeling of, say, one's own breathing is quite distinct from the judgment or opinion that one is breathing. For an asthmatic patient the feeling of his breathing is likely to be unpleasant or even painful; his opinion, on the other hand, if it is an opinion, that he is breathing, or that he is breathing painfully, is neither unpleasant nor painful. Moreover, whereas those feelings are felt in the chest and the throat of the patient, his thought that he is breathing, or that he is in pain, is not felt in any part of his body. Thoughts, in fact, are not "felt" or "experienced" at all. Again, although we may grant that from the idea that one is breathing one can conclude to one's existence "very well," no such conclusion follows from a mere sensation, for the simple reason that it is not a proposition from which one could conclude something or other.

For, notice, the idea that one is in pain, or feels hunger, or perceives heat, light, or sound, is a genuine proposition, which can be expressed in speech by simply saying, "I am in pain," "I

31 *Meditation VI*: AT VII, 78; HR I, 190.
32 Letter, March 1638: AT II, 37 (my italics).

feel hot," "I see flashes of light," and so forth. The natural expression of the sensations themselves, however, are cries, gestures, postures, grimaces, and the like. Of course, I can describe such sensations in words—by saying, for example, "I have a burning sensation in my stomach"—but this will be the expression of a thought, namely, that I have a burning sensation in my stomach, and not of the burning sensation itself. And you, the listener, will understand what I said, believe it or disbelieve it, without being committed to the absurdity of believing any sensation. To put it in another way, the thought that I have a certain sensation is a construction out of concepts, and as such an object for the understanding (yours and mine), but the sensation itself is not conceptualised, not something to be understood; it is felt, felt by me and not by you.

Speaking of concepts, "ideas" in the narrow sense, it is worth remarking that Descartes persistently confuses sensations of a certain kind with the idea of such sensations: pain with the idea of pain, the experiences of light and sound with the ideas of light and sound. This confusion leads to the empiricist attempt to construe all ideas, or most ideas, out of sensory elements—a tendency against which Descartes himself fulminates in his replies to Hobbes' objections (*Reply III*) and elsewhere.

7. In giving the analysis of the concept of sensation, which we reproduced above, Descartes mentions "those judgments which we have . . . been accustomed to pass about things external to us" on the third level. Now what about such perceptual judgments as the ones just discussed or the ones Descartes himself gives in *Meditation II*, to wit, "It seems to me that I see light [videre videor; il me semble que je voy], that I hear noise, and that I feel heat." [33] It seems to me, on the basis of the

[33] *Meditation II: AT VII, 29; HR I, 153.*

texts quoted above, that he banishes such thoughts to the limbo of the second level to be mixed up there with the sensations themselves. Such an admixture of judgments to the "raw" sensations would indeed account for his view that in sensation "some kind of intellection is comprised."

There are passages, however, in which he seems to draw a distinction. In *Reply III* he says: "It is self-evident that . . . it is one thing to see a man running [videre hominem currentem], another to affirm to oneself that one sees it [sibi ipsi affirmare se illum videre], an act that needs no language [quod fit sine voce]." [34] From the context it is obvious that by "see a man running" he does not mean seeing as a mere organic process (level one) but as an inner experience (level two), since this particular objection (Objection VI) deals with the various forms of thought. Yet, as we see here, he distinguishes this seeing from the subsequent judgment. One should keep in mind, however, that this judgment is an "objective" one (I see a man running); thus the text still leaves open the possibility that the experience referred to embodies, or is identical with, a "subjective" judgment of the form "It seems to me that I see a man running."

In the *Principles* there is an equally puzzling text: "For if I say I see, or I walk, I therefore am, and if by seeing and walking I mean the action of my eyes or my legs, which is the work of my body, my conclusion is not absolutely certain; . . . But if I mean only to talk of my sensation, or my consciously seeming to see or to walk [de ipso sensu sive conscientia videndi aut ambulandi], it becomes quite true because my assertion now refers only to my mind, which alone is concerned with my feeling or thinking that I see and I walk [quae sola sentit sive

[34] *Reply III* (Obj. VI): AT VII, 182–183; HR II, 69.

cogitat se videre aut ambulare]." [35] In this second case the assertion "I see" or "I walk" is supposed to refer to "my sensation, or my consciously seeming to see or to walk." Therefore that assertion is to be paraphrased as, "It seems to me that I see or that I walk." Consequently, since this assertion cannot refer to itself, my sensation, or my consciously seeming to see or to walk, appears to be distinct even from such a subjective judgment. Yet, again, the closing line of the text seems to confuse feeling with thinking by juxtaposing the two and by assigning to both a propositional object—that is, that I see or that I walk.

Finally, consider the following passage from *Meditation VI*, in which Descartes tries to show that the soul is intermingled with the body: "For if that were not the case, when my body is hurt, I, who am merely a thinking thing, should not feel pain, for I should perceive this wound by the understanding only, just as the sailor perceives by sight when something is damaged in his vessel; and when my body has need of drink or food, I should clearly understand the fact without being warned of it by confused feelings of hunger and thirst." [36] Now these confused feelings are surely not identical with any judgment of the understanding, not even with such trivial ones as "I feel pain (hunger, etc.)." Notice, incidentally, that these feelings are supposed to warn me, the thinking thing. But if they themselves are thought, then who warns whom? One part of the mind warns the other? This Descartes could not allow, for to him the mind is a simple substance, not composed of parts or accidents.[37] What he said above about imagination, is true of sensation too: "Even if I did not possess it I should doubtless

[35] *Principles*, I, 9: AT VIII, 7–8; HR I, 222.
[36] *Meditation VI*: AT VII, 81; HR I, 192.
[37] See, e.g., *Meditation VI*: AT VII, 86; HR I, 196, and Synopsis of the *Meditations*: AT VII, 14; HR I, 141.

ever remain the same as I now am." [38] It seems to follow, at least from this text, that mere sensation, or feeling, is not really a mode of the mind, that it is not thought after all.

8. Nevertheless, since he is unable to say what distinguishes true thought from mere experience, the latter remains for Descartes "a certain confused mode of thought." [39] Given this, allowing experience in animals would be tantamount to an attribution of minds to them, with all the resultant privileges, such as rights, duties, immortality, and so forth. In the letter to Henry More he writes: "It is more reasonable to make earthworms, flies, caterpillars, and the rest of the animals move as machines do, than to endow them with immortal souls." [40] We can add a third possibility: animals may have feelings and sensations without having thoughts—may have a soul, if you like, but not a mind. This, of course, is the view of the tradition and of the common sense of mankind.

Descartes' predecessors, the scholastic philosophers, did not encounter any difficulty in attributing sensations and a sensitive soul to animals. The reason is easy to see. Operating in the Aristotelian framework, they distinguished the senses from the understanding by their respective "formal" objects: qualities of concrete individuals for the senses, abstract essences (quidditates) for the understanding. Therefore, only the understanding appeared to be something nonmaterial, thus possibly separable and immortal. The aspect of immediate awareness, or consciousness, of all these operations had been neglected, except in the Augustinian tradition—nearly defunct in Descartes' intellectual environment. Now one aspect of the Cartesian

38 *Meditation* VI: AT VII, 73; HR I, 186.
39 *Ibid.*: AT VII, 81; HR I, 192.
40 Letter (to Morus), Feb. 1649: AT V, 277; Eaton, p. 359.

revolution precisely consisted in the focusing of an almost exclusive attention on the manner rather than on the object of these inner operations; immediate awareness, in fact, became Descartes' sole criterion of thought. This insistence on immediacy, together with the lack of attention toward the respective objects of these operations, accounts for Descartes' fear of attributing experience to beasts. The approach taken in this book, stressing the propositional nature of all real thought, reinstates the Aristotelian and scholastic distinction between the senses and the understanding, albeit on a somewhat different basis. Animals may feel without thinking, as we humans often do.

9. Is it possible to feel without thinking? Can one have experiences without corresponding perceptual judgments?

The problem arises as follows. We have seen in Chapter III that all thoughts are tied to the subject via the mental frames (mental acts or states) in which one entertains propositions. As in speech the subject of all illocutions is the "I" of the speaker, so in thought the subject of all mental acts and states is the "I" of the thinker. As Kant said it, "The proposition 'I think . . .' contains the form of each and every judgment of understanding." [41] The "I" is, as it were, the point of intersection of all thoughts that constitute an individual mind, a particular "thinking thing." This "I," moreover, is by no means a mere bracket that holds together an assorted set of propositions. For these propositions, at least a significant portion of them, are marked by the features of "subjectivity" discussed in Chapter IV: the self is no mere bundle of propositions, it is the common perspective or referential coherence of these propositions, reflecting the spatiotemporal location and continuity of one's body; it is a microcosm, a "living mirror of the uni-

[41] *Critique of Pure Reason*, B. 406.

verse." [42] The subjectivity, finally, of the content of one's mind is clearly contrasted with the objective ideal, the world of facts. Then it is not obvious how feelings and sensations can belong to a subject, how they can be part of an individual consciousness. Pains, perceptions of heat and light, and so forth are not propositions, have no element of reference; consequently they do not warrant a distinction between the subjective and the objective. In a word, they are not intrinsically marked as mine or thine.

"But—surely—I feel what I feel." True—but notice that you can also say, "It hurts," "My stomach aches," and "My scalp itches." On the other hand, one never says, "It believes," "My head decided," and so forth. Sensations and feelings, unlike beliefs, wishes, and intentions, are, in a sense, "outside" of us: they are "there" to be noticed or ignored. Moreover, since they can be located in space, they belong, in a sense again, to the "res extensa" rather than to the "res cogitans." After all, they have many attributes that characterize spatiotemporal events and processes: they occur, begin, last and end, increase or diminish in intensity (they can be measured), or even move, as shooting pains do. Mental images, too, are at least perceived as spread out in space. None of these things is true of real thoughts, except in a metaphorical sense.

If, following the hint of etymology (*con-scire*), consciousness be defined as the totality of one's thoughts (at a given moment), then sensations and feelings do not enter one's consciousness until by noticing or being aware of them one forms or entertains a perceptual judgment. If this is true, then we must agree with Descartes that animals, strictly speaking, cannot be conscious of their sensations and other experiences. This

[42] Leibniz, *Monadology*, 56: *Leibniz Selections* (ed. P. P. Wiener), p. 544.

does not mean, however, that we must agree with him in regarding them as mere automata—that is, as having sensations only in the sense of undergoing certain physiological changes. For, clearly, in noticing or being aware of our sensations we might not, and by and large do not, notice or are aware of the corresponding physiological changes. People noticed their pains before the rise of physiology. What we notice, therefore, is neither the physiological change, nor, obviously, the act of noticing itself, but something distinct from both.

Thus we are back with Descartes' schema of three levels: physiological states, "raw" sensations (sense-data, if you like), and judgments (subjective or objective) consequent upon these sensations. Humans operate on all three levels, animals on the first and the second.

10. It is interesting to realize that the characteristic examples that Descartes himself offers to illustrate automatic behavior are, in fact, examples of behavior without thought in our sense, rather than instances of behavior without thought in his sense, that is without accompanying experience.

In *Reply IV* he writes:

The greater part of our motions do not depend on the mind at all. Such are the beatings of the heart, the digestion of our food, nutrition, respiration when we are asleep and even walking, singing and similar acts when we are awake, if performed without the mind attending to them. When a man in falling thrusts out his hand to save his head he does that without his reason counselling him so to act, but merely because the sight of the impending fall penetrating to his brain, drives the animal spirits into the nerves in the manner necessary for this motion, and for producing it without the mind's desiring it, and as though it were the working of a machine.[43]

[43] *Reply IV*: AT VII, 229–230; HR II, 103–104.

In this text Descartes confuses situations of at least three different types. Heartbeat, digestion, and the like belong to the first type: physiological processes (normally) without concomitant feelings. Owing to the lack of such experience one cannot notice, or become aware of these processes at all. The second type is that of "mindless" walking, singing, and the like. Actions of this type are clearly accompanied by certain experiences (visual, tactual, auditory), which one can notice or become aware of, even though one might not be aware of them all the time. Think of the difference between the condition of a man deep in thought, pacing up and down in a familiar room, and the condition of a blind man doing the same. The former, I claim, has visual experiences but does not pay attention to them, whereas the latter has no such experiences at all. The "reflex" of the falling man, finally, illustrates the third type: an action not controlled by the mind. But is "the sight of the impending fall" a mere physiological happening, as Descartes suggests, or is it accompanied by experience? Certainly the latter. Compare this situation with merely mechanical reflexes, such as the contraction of one's pupil while asleep and reflexes in the digestive tract.

There is a parallel passage in the letter to the Marquis of Newcastle: "It often happens that we walk and that we eat without thinking at all [sans penser en aucune façon] upon what we are doing; and it is so much without the use of our reason [raison] that we repel things which harm us, and ward off blows struck at us." [44] Without thinking, without the use of reason, I grant; without sensations and perceptions, I deny. Once more, Descartes equivocates on the notion of thinking: by pointing out that these actions occur without thought in the strict sense (reason), he pretends to show that they occur with-

[44] *Letter* (to the Marquis of Newcastle), Nov. 1646: AT IV, 573; Eaton 355.

out thought in his own extended sense, that is without sensation. But the absentminded man is not a machine, and the animal is not an automaton.

One more passage from a reply to Burman: "The body affects the soul to the extent of interfering with it; we experience this in ourselves: when stabbed by a needle or some other instrument, this affects us so much that we cannot think about anything else." [45] The man on the rack might not be able to think about anything else, granted. Is it because he is thinking about the rack, or his pain, without intermission? Not at all. Most likely he cannot think about anything at all, and this because of the excruciating pain he feels. Extreme agony, heat of passion, rapture of the senses, and so forth, may indeed suppress all thought and reduce a man to the level of the brutes. And, since the self is essentially the subject of thoughts, such a man is said to be "beside himself" (with pain, rage, etc.): the "I" is in abeyance.

11. There seems to be another way of being "beside oneself." If it makes sense what the mystics say, then it appears that the contemplation of a timeless and supramundane realm (or of the world in that context) might lead to "transport" or "ecstasy": the subjective perspective of our wordly thoughts is missing, and the "I" is suspended once more. "The contemplation of the world sub specie aeterni is its contemplation as a limited whole. The feeling of the world as a limited whole is the mystical feeling." [46] Man attempts to view the world not from the "inside," not as a definite part of it, which would create a perspective, but from the "outside," as it is in itself— from the "point of view" of an angel or God.

Animals are not conscious because they have no thoughts.

[45] Replies (to Burman), April 1648: AT V, 150.
[46] Wittgenstein, *Tractatus*, 6.45.

Res Cogitans

Angels, if they exist, may have thoughts, but these will not individuate them, since they have no body; consequently their thoughts will not be affected by a spatiotemporal perspective. They must be, as the Thomists say, unique in a species, and these "specific" individuals distinct according to the "perfection" of their thoughts. We may recall, from Chapter IV, that perspective is not the only source of subjectivity; ignorance is another. My concept of transfinite numbers is distinct from Cantor's concept of such numbers, not because of a difference in perspective, but because of a difference in the degree of comprehension. Finally, in the "omniscient" God the very distinction between the subjective and the objective must vanish, "and the act of thinking will be one with the object of thought (καὶ ἡ νόησις τῷ νοουμένῳ μία)." [47]

In making these remarks I do not imply that God and angels exist. I do not even raise the question of their existence. I am interested in the concept of an angel and of God, because these concepts seem to delimitate the notion of man as it were from above, as the concept of an animal does from below. If you say that the concepts are themselves inconsistent, I reply that you may be right, but it has to be shown. Think of the "concept" of the largest prime—and remember that our concepts, even if they are "clear and distinct," are open to development, or, if they only appear in the guise of such an idea, to defeasance.

Ideas

12. Returning now to thoughts in the strict sense of the word, Descartes divides them as follows:

Of my thoughts some are, so to speak, images of the things, and to these alone is the title 'idea' properly applied; examples are my

[47] Aristotle, *Met. XII*, 1075a.

thought of a man or of a chimera, of heaven, of an angel, or (even) of God. But other thoughts possess other forms as well. For example in willing, fearing, approving, denying, though I always perceive something as the subject of the action of my mind, yet by this action I always add something else to the idea which I have of that thing [aliquid etiam amplius quam istius rei similitudinem cogitatione complector]; and of the thoughts of this kind some are called volitions or affections and others judgments.[48]

He goes on to say that truth and falsity are not to be found in the simple ideas, nor in the actions of the will or affection, but only in judgments.

At the first blush this passage appears to be but a repetition of the scholastic commonplace (derived from Aristotle) that only judgments (i.e., the objects of *intellectus componens et dividens*), and not ideas (i.e., the object of *apprehensio simplex*) are true or false. Looking closer, however, we realize that Descartes must have meant more than that. First of all, his suggestion that such operations as willing and fearing have a structure similar to that of judgments goes beyond the scholastic precedents. Moreover, it is clear that "the subject of the action of my mind" cannot be just an idea, and the "something else" that the mind adds to that subject by any one of these actions cannot be just another idea. Take denial, which he explicitly mentions. The man who denies God does not deny an idea; he denies the proposition that God exists. And what he adds to this proposition is not another idea, but the "force" or "mental frame" of his dissent or disagreement.

This becomes quite clear in *Meditation IV*. He writes:

It comes to pass that I *doubt* whether this thinking nature which is in me . . . differs from this corporeal nature, or whether both are simply the same thing; and I here suppose that I do not yet

[48] *Meditation III:* AT VII, 37; HR I, 159.

know any reason to persuade me to adopt the one belief rather than the other. From this it follows that I am entirely indifferent as to which of the two I *affirm* or *deny*, or even whether I *abstain from forming any judgment* in the matter [nihil de ea re iudicandum].[49]

Obviously, the object of doubt, affirmation, and denial are propositions which the mind may entertain *before* affirming or denying them—that is, before forming a positive or negative judgment. For that matter, not even the famous rule in the *Discourse*, "that the things which we conceive very clearly and distinctly are all true," [50] would make much sense if these clear and distinct "things" were mere concepts rather than propositions.

Now since, as we just saw, Descartes assigns the same structure to such a variety of acts as willing, fearing, approving, denying, and desiring, we can safely conclude that he makes a distinction between the content and the form of a mental act in much the same way as we have distinguished between the proposition and the mental frame. With the same consequence too: truth or falsity is a function of the "something" added to the proposition, in a "judgment" to him and in some more specific act in the domain of "apprehensives" and "putatives" to us.

13. The limitations of his training, as well as the background of the audience he addresses, particularly in the *Meditations*, forces Descartes to express this insight in the scholastic jargon. In *Meditation III* he gets by with the familiar distinction between ideas and judgments; in *Meditation IV*, however, where these concepts would be too plainly inadequate, he invokes the

49 *Meditation IV:* AT VII, 59; HR I, 176 (my italics).
50 *Discourse:* AT VI, 33; HR I, 102.

Descartes' Res Cogitans

"will" to do the trick: it is the will that adds the affirmative or negative force to the proposition, grasped by the understanding, to make it into a judgment. For nothing but the will is available in the scholastic arsenal besides the understanding to handle the higher functions of man. His recourse to the will is beautifully described in the *Notes against a Programme*:

> When I saw that, over and above perception, which is required as a basis for judgement, there must needs be affirmation, or negation, to constitute the form of judgement, and that it is frequently open to us to withhold our assent, even if we perceive a thing, I referred the act of judging, which consists in nothing but *assent*, i.e. affirmation or negation, not to the perception of the understanding, but to the determination of the will.[51]

Thus, in his concern to preserve the scholastic terminology, he ends up with a highly "unscholastic" claim: "For by the understanding alone I (neither assent nor deny anything but) only apprehend the ideas of things as to which I can form judgment." [52]

He is out on a limb, and not only because of his unorthodoxy. For if the structure of judging and willing is similar, as he claimed in *Meditation III*, and if the "something else" added to the idea in a judgment comes from the will, then the question arises, whence does the "something else" come from in an act of the will? From a "superwill"—the first step in an infinite regress?

What he should have said, of course, and what he does in fact imply in a number of passages, is that it is the "I" itself that supplies the particular force to all the mental acts, to

[51] AT VIII, 363; HR I, 446. Incidentally, the fact that he often calls the "things" we affirm or deny in our judgments ideas rather than propositions should not disturb us in view of his remark: "nomen ideae . . . ego vero ad id omne quod cogitatur, extendo" (*Reply* V: AT VIII, 366).
[52] *Meditation IV*: AT VII, 56; HR I, 174.

judgments, doubts, intentions, volitions, and so forth, alike. But this thesis smacks of a still greater heresy: the soul acting by itself and not through any faculty, which, to the tradition, is the privilege of God alone.

If I am not mistaken, this is the explanation of Descartes' uncharacteristic "voluntarism" expressed in *Meditation IV*. When he says things like, "He has given me a will more ample than my understanding, for since the will consists only of one single element, and is so to speak indivisible, it appears that its nature is such that nothing can be abstracted from it (without destroying it),"[53] he really speaks, or *should* speak, not of the will but of the self: simple, indivisible, and sovereign, the "transcendental" subject of all thoughts. As we shall see, Descartes had this idea of the self, implied in the *Cogito* argument and made palatable to scholastic readers in his theory of "modes" (which are "not quite" the self, but more than mere accidents), yet, for obvious religious reasons, he never had the courage to acknowledge it and to abandon the doctrine of the soul as a "substance" interacting with other substances in the world. That final step remained for Kant to take.

Even so, Descartes broadens the terminology: he speaks of understanding, doubting, and willing (and imagining and perceiving) as "manners of thought [façons de penser],"[54] "kinds of thought [especes de pensées],"[55] "forms [formae]" of the mind,[56] and, of course, "modes [modi]" of the mind.

14. As for ideas in the narrow sense, that is concepts, I have little to say, since on this point I am in almost complete agreement with Descartes.

[53] *Ibid.*: AT VII, 60; HR I, 177.
[54] Letter (to Mersenne), Apr. 1637: AT I, 366.
[55] Letter (to P. [Gibieuf]), Jan. 1642: AT III, 478.
[56] *Reply IV*: AT VII, 223; HR II, 99.

Descartes' Res Cogitans

I begin by noting his insistence that ideas are distinct both from mental images and from words pronounced or mentally evoked. At the beginning of *Meditation VI* he carefully distinguishes conception from imagination, and in his answers to Hobbes's objections (*Reply III*) he gets "tired of repeating" [57] that we do have an idea of God and of angels; [58] that the proper idea of the sun is exactly the one "derived from the astronomical reasonings, i.e. is elicited from certain notions that are innate in me"; [59] that "in reasoning we unite not names but the things signified by the names" [60] (i.e., "pure mental concepts" [61]); and that the act of affirming something to oneself is an "act that needs no language." [62]

Some ideas may show a high degree of complexity. Think of the idea of the chiliagon, mentioned at the beginning of *Meditation VI*, or the astronomical concept of the sun. To have an idea of a chiliagon is to know what kind of figure it is; to have an astronomical concept of the sun is to know what the sun is in terms of astronomy. Accordingly, the expression of these ideas will amount to a complex definition. This conclusion is in perfect agreement with our findings in Chapter VI: an idea is an open proposition, often a very complex open proposition. We also agree with Descartes that the ultimate elements of this complexity are native ideas, "elicited from certain notions that are innate in me."

This conceptual "purity" is the property of clear and distinct ideas only. "Confused" ideas, such as the prescientific notions of taste, smell, sound, color, cold, and heat, as well as such ideas as that of a lion or a horse will contain an abundance of sensory elements precisely because "their natures are not wholly in-

[57] *Reply III*: AT VII, 189; HR II, 74.
[58] *Ibid*: AT VII, 181; HR II, 67.   [59] *Ibid*.: AT VII, 184; HR II, 70.
[60] *Ibid*.: AT VII, 178; HR II, 66.   [61] *Ibid*.
[62] *Ibid*.: AT VII, 183; HR II, 69.

171

telligible to us." [63] Yet, as the two ideas of the sun illustrate, such concepts may be replaced by clear and distinct ones (and many of them have been so replaced since Descartes' time). Thus although he regards the admixture of the sensory elements as a likely source of error in thinking,[64] he acknowledges its role in the formation of confused ideas. Moreover, he also admits that even in some "clear and distinct" domains, notably in geometry, imagination at least may come to the aid of the understanding: "The body, that is to say, extension . . . can be known by the understanding alone, but much better by the understanding aided by the imagination [par l'entendement aidé de l'imagination]." [65]

15. The theory of innate ideas has emerged in our own discussion as the key to the notion of understanding, which, in turn, is the pivotal concept in any adequate account of speech and language. The same theory is also the cornerstone of Descartes' whole philosophy. When he sets out to give a brief outline of his system to a layman (Elizabeth), he begins as follows:

In the first place, I assume that there are in us certain primitive notions [notions primitives], which are like some originals, on the pattern of which we form all the other ideas [sur le patron desquels nous formons toutes les autres connoisances] . . . being, number, duration, which apply to all we can conceive; . . . for the body . . . extension, and what follows from it, (namely) shape and motion; and for the soul, . . . thought, in which the perceptions of the understanding and the inclinations of the will are included.[66]

The first two headings in this list, the "common" notions and the "corporeal" ideas, have been recognized as somehow fundamental to human understanding since Plato's time. The

[63] *Reply I:* AT VII, 117; HR II, 20.
[64] *Principles,* I, 66ff: AT VIII, 32ff; HR I, 247ff.
[65] Letter (to Elizabeth), June, 1643: AT III, 692.
[66] Letter (to Elizabeth), May, 1643: AT III, 665.

recognition of the third group, the "mental" notions, is quite original with Descartes. He lays great stress upon these "purely intellectual" concepts "which our understanding apprehends by means of a certain inborn light [lumen . . . ingenitum], and without the aid of any corporeal image," since "it is impossible to construct any corporeal idea which shall represent to us what knowledge is, what doubt is, what ignorance, and likewise what the action of the will is, which may be called volition, and the like; yet we know all these things, and so easily, that it is sufficient for us to be endowed with reason to know them".[67] It is interesting to notice that he refers to these ideas by means of the same turn of phrase that we used in speaking about concepts: "what knowledge [doubt, etc.] is [quid sit cognitio]." The only major category missing in Descartes' list is the group of notions corresponding to speech: what it is to state, to ask, to order, to promise, and so on—in a word, what it is to say something.

He remains on the level of thought. Yet the "analysis" he offers concerning one of these mental concepts reminds one strongly of Austin's treatment of presuppositions, and even more strongly of some recent work by the generative semanticists: "If Socrates says he doubts everything, it follows necessarily that he knows this at least—that he doubts. Likewise he knows that something can be either true or false, and so on, for all these consequences necessarily attach to the nature of doubt [naturae dubitationis necessario annexa sunt]." [68]

16. In what sense are Descartes' innate ideas innate? I wish to go into this matter a bit more extensively not only because of its bearing upon the current controversies provoked by Noam

---

[67] *Rules for Direction*, XII: AT X, 419; HR I, 41 (I deviate slightly from HR).
[68] *Ibid.*: AT X, 421; HR I, 43.

Res Cogitans

Chomsky's renewal of "Cartesian linguistics," [69] but also to do justice to Descartes himself, whose doctrine on this point has been distorted beyond recognition by most of his commentators and critics.

It is true that he calls these ideas, and the principles they engender, innate (innatae), "inborn in our minds [mentibus nostris ingenitae]" [70]. Yet he regards it as a "slanderous imputation" that he ever held that these ideas are innate *in actu*, that is, in a fully blown, conscious form: "That these ideas are *actual* [actuales], or that they are some kind of species different from the faculty of thought I never wrote nor concluded [nec unquam scripsisse nec cogitasse]." [71] All he ever claimed, he adds, is that they are *potentially* present at the inception of the soul. The actual-potential distinction is, of course, scholastic talk, and, as we have found on another occasion, Descartes has no luck with scholastic jargon. For, given the normal sense of this distinction, to say that these ideas are potentially present in the soul merely means that the soul is capable of developing them in no matter what fashion, due to the influence of no matter what agency. To use the trite example, the statue is potentially present in the block of marble before the sculptor starts his work. In this sense any normal human infant has the idea of doughnuts, filter-tips, and home runs potentially at birth, since he is capable of developing them later on. Still, as Aristotle has insisted, potency is not nothing, since a plant or a newborn porcupine does not have such ability.

But this is not what Descartes wants to say, and when he

---

[69] See his *Cartesian Linguistics* and *Language and Mind* and the relevant papers in Sidney Hook (ed.), *Language and Philosophy*.

[70] Letter (to Mersenne), April 1630: AT I, 81.

[71] *Notes against a Programme*: AT VIII, 366; HR I, 448. Notice, incidentally, the parallelism between thought and writing in the last words.

leaves the scholastic terms alone, he says it quite clearly in the same work:

When I observed the existence in me of certain thoughts which proceeded, *not from extraneous objects nor from the determination of my will, but solely from the faculty of thinking* which is within me, then . . . I termed [them] 'innate'. In the same sense we say that in some families generosity is innate, in others certain diseases like gout or gravel, not that on this account the babes of these families suffer from the diseases in their mother's womb, but because they are born with a certain disposition or propensity [cum quadam dispositione sive facultate] for contracting them.[72]

Again, in *Reply III* he writes:

When I say that an idea is innate in us (or imprinted in our souls by nature), I do not mean that it is always present to us. This would make no idea innate. I mean merely that we possess the faculty of eliciting this idea [facultatem illam eliciendi; la faculté de la produire].[73]

Thus the point is not that the soul is capable of forming these ideas, but that it can do so from its own resources. Not like the block of marble or the piece of wood, out of which anything may be hacked out, but like a living tree that is natively predisposed to develop certain very specific and very definite type of leaves, flowers, and fruits. Of course, even the tree needs soil, water, and light to do so, as the child needs some minimal environment. Yet the specification of those flowers, and these ideas, are not determined by the soil, or the environment, but by an innate programme spelled out in the chromosomes of the tree, and—though Descartes would not agree—of the child.

[72] *Ibid.*: AT VIII, 358; HR I, 442 (my italics).
[73] *Reply III*: AT VII, 189; AT IX, 147; HR II, 73. For the sake of accuracy I changed the last line of the translation (*eliciting* instead of *summoning up*).

Leibniz—far more articulate than Descartes—explicitly re-jects the opinion.

which claimed that when it is said that innate ideas are implicitly in the mind, this must mean simply that it has the faculty of know-ing them; for I have shown that in addition to this, it has the faculty of finding them in itself [la faculté de les trouver en soy], and the disposition to approve of them when it thinks of them as it should.[74]

It is not, therefore, a naked faculty which consists in the mere pos-sibility of understanding them; it is a disposition, an aptitude, a preformation, which determines our soul.[75]

And then he gives the analogy of the marble with the outline of the statue already marked out in it.

17. How do these ideas that are "potentially" ("virtually" would be a better word, if one still wanted to use scholastic terms) in the soul, become "actual," conscious objects of thought? There is an amazingly Platonic—and, at the same time, amazingly modern—passage in *Reply* V dealing with this problem:

When first in infancy we see a triangular figure depicted on paper, this figure cannot show us how a real triangle ought to be conceived, in the way in which geometricians consider it, because the true tri-angle is contained in this figure, just as the statue of Mercury is contained in a rough block of wood. But because we already possess within us the idea of a true triangle, and it can be more easily con-ceived by our mind than the more complex figure of the triangle drawn on paper, we, therefore, when we see that composite figure, apprehend not itself, but rather the authentic triangle [visa ista figura composita, non illam ipsam, sed potius verum triangulum apprehendimus]. This is exactly the same as when we look at a piece of paper on which little strokes have been drawn with ink to

---

[74] *New Essays*, Book I, Chapter I, §21; Wiener, 406.   [75] *Ibid.*, §11.

represent a man's face; for the idea produced in us in this way is not so much of the lines of the sketch as of the man. But this could not have happened unless the human face had been known to us by other means [nisi facies . . . aliunde nota fuisset], and we had been more accustomed to think of it [magis assueti de illa . . . cogitare] than of those minute lines.[76]

The two cases, of course, are not "exactly the same." We see the human face in the line drawing because the shape is familiar to us: that *Gestalt* is imprinted in our memory. Incidentally, such an imprinting can be innate too: newly hatched chickens "recognize" feed grain. The child, however, sees the crude triangular drawing as (the representation of) a real triangle not because this figure is "familiar" to him on the account of memory or innate imprinting, but because it "can be more easily conceived" in terms of such native ideas as straight line and angle. There is a "clear and distinct" idea of a triangle, whch can be defined and from which theorems can be derived. This is not true of the shape of the human face; it is not a simple construct out of simple elements. It cannot be *understood* in the way the notion of a triangle is understood by the uninstructed child in *Meno*.

In a similar way, in learning the language the child comes to recognize illocutionary forces, syntactic structures, and semantic content in the scattered and often decayed scraps of conversation he is exposed to, as their intelligibility progressively opens up to him with the maturing of his own native conceptual apparatus.[77]

The child, I claimed, sees the clumsy drawing as a triangle, because this figure is something understandable to him. Need-

[76] AT VII, 382; HR II, 227–228. The passage "just as the statue . . ." alludes, of course, to the medieval doctrine of abstraction.

[77] See some recent psychological findings in the volumes by E. H. Lennenberg, and by F. Smith and G. A. Miller, listed in the Bibliography.

less to say, his understanding is not complete. There are many things that he does not know about the nature of triangles. Nor does he know everything about the human face, we may add, even if he is already able to recognize its shape. In either case, he can learn more. But there the similarity ends. What he learns about the human face, he learns from experience, his own or his elders'. Not so with the triangle: "When I derive [eruam] from an innate idea what it implicitly contains, but hitherto remained unnoticed to me, e.g., from the idea of a triangle that its three angles equal two right angles . . . etc. [I apply] the most perfect form of demonstration, namely the one in which the very definition of the thing functions as the middle term." [78] To put it in less forbidding language: in trying to refine and develop my understanding of such things as triangles, I do not have to consult the data of experience (acquired by me or other people), for all there is to know about them is derivable from a system of concepts, and—perhaps—pure intuition. The same is true of the notions of mathematics. As for logic, ethics, and the kind of "psychology" or "metaphysics" we are doing in these pages, this is still more so: not even pure intuition (of space and time, that is) is relevant to our understanding of such concepts as truth, necessity, entailment, duty, intention, statement, and the like.

18. For the reasons I mentioned in Chapter I, Descartes did not feel a need to discuss language *ex professo* or in great detail. To him, as to the schoolmen before him and to his followers later on, speech is the expression of thought. Animals use no language, he argues, and thus they have no thoughts; but we talk, because we think. Hence the ability to speak constitutes the true specific difference (*vera differentia*) between man and

[78] Letter (to Mersenne), June 1641: AT III, 383.

beast: the soul is *res cogitans*, but man, the composite of soul and body, who can be contrasted with the beasts, is *res loquens.*[79]

The relation between the exercise of real speech (*vera loquela*) and the presence of thought is a necessary one. Descartes is most emphatic on this point. "We could not express anything by our words, [par nos paroles], understanding what we are saying, without that very fact making it certain that we have the idea of the thing which these words signify," he writes to Mersenne,[80] and he includes the Latin version of the same sentence in the short compendium of his system appended to *Reply II*.[81] This claim is not circular. We have pretty reliable criteria for telling whether somebody merely parrots words or knows what he is saying. In the second case, his words are like to be *à propos* some circumstance or context. If we are not sure, we can ask him to paraphrase. Finally, Hegel's "test" is almost infallible: "Surely a man knows a text really by heart only when he does not need to attach any sense to the words; accordingly, he will recite the text thus memorized without [natural] stress or intonation. For the correct intonation follows the sense of the passage; but if meaning and comprehension were to accompany the recital, they would interfere with the mechanical sequence and disturb the recital." [82] When, in reading aloud, we reach a passage that escapes our understanding, our intonation flattens out even if we keep on pronouncing the

[79] See footnote 23, above. The context, *"eamque idcirco pro vera inter homines et bruta differentia sumere licet,"* indicates that he uses *difference* in the technical sense, as *differentia specifica*.

[80] July 1641: AT III, 393.

[81] *Arguments . . . in Geometrical Fashion:* AT VII, 160; HR II, 52.

[82] *Enzyklopädie*, §463. I translate freely, since I use Hegel's idea, not his authority. Incidentally a rhythmic pattern of intonation, divorced from meaning, is a powerful aid in memorizing texts. Think of prosody.

words. The child "rattles off" his prayers if he does not understand, or does not care about, what they mean.

Speech without thought is not true speech, and thought itself is not verbal. According to Descartes, internal judgments "need no language." "Moreover, in reasoning we unite not names but the things signified by the names; and I marvel that the opposite can occur to anyone. For who doubts whether a Frenchman and a German are able to arrive at identical conclusions about the same things [eadem plane iisdem de rebus possint ratiocinari], though they conceive entirely different words [cum tamen verba concipiant plane diversa]?" [83]

The meaning of words consist in their relation to thoughts:

In learning a language one joins the letters or the pronunciation of certain words, which are material things, to their signification, which are thoughts [avec leurs significations, qui sont des pensées]; so that afterwards, when one perceives the same words, one conceives the same things; and when one conceives the same things, one remembers the same words.[84]

In more detail:

When I am told that the sound [vocem] R-E-X signifies the supreme power and I commit it to my memory, and when I recall this meaning [significationem] later on, this certainly happens by intellectual memory, since there is no affinity between these three letters [literas] and their meaning.[85]

There is a very early letter of Descartes, written to Mersenne, in which he discusses the merits of a recently proposed "new language," and adds some observations of his own. In view of the rarity of Cartesian texts dealing with language, I hope to

[83] *Reply III:* AT VII, 178–179; HR II, 66 (the translation of the phrases quoted in the original is mine).
[84] Letter (to Chanut), Feb. 1647: AT IV, 604.
[85] Replies (to Burman), April 1648: AT V, 150.

be excused for quoting at length from this little gem of "Cartesian linguistics."

I think moreover, that one could add to this a device to compose both the primitive words and the characters of this language; in such a way that it could be taught in very short time and in an orderly fashion; that is to say, by establishing an order among all the thoughts that can enter the human mind, much the same way as there is one among the numbers; as one can learn in a day to name all the numbers up to infinity, and to write them, in an unknown language, yet these are, after all, an infinity of different words, one could do the same with respect to all the other words that are necessary to express anything that may enter a man's mind. . . . The invention of this language presupposes true philosophy, since it is otherwise impossible to enumerate all the thoughts of man, to put them in order, and to distinguish them in a clear and simple manner.[86]

It also presupposes a set of "simple ideas, which are in man's mind [en l'imagination], from which all his thoughts are composed." [87]

This appears to be (even in the original) somewhat hastily written (think of the glaring *obiter dictum: en l'imagination*), yet the central idea is crystal clear: Descartes envisions a "generative" grammar, and semantics, for his language, which would correspond to the generative structure of thought. He did not realize, of course, that a natural language comes close to this ideal. So he complains: "The words we possess have somewhat confused meanings, to which people's minds are accustomed through long use, and this is the reason why they hardly understood anything perfectly." [88] And, in a much later work: "Because we attach all our conceptions to words for the expression of them by speech . . . we can scarcely conceive of

[86] Letter (to Mersenne), Nov. 1629: AT I, 80–81.
[87] *Ibid.*　[88] *Ibid.*

anything so distinctly as to be able to separate completely that which we conceive from the words chosen to express the same. In this way most men apply their attention to words rather than things, and this is the cause of their frequently giving their assent to terms which they do not understand." [89]

These rather pessimistic remarks should be read in conjunction with such optimistic texts as the one already quoted about Germans and Frenchmen being able to have the same thoughts despite the alleged inability to abstract ideas from words. After all, as Descartes writes in another letter to Mersenne, "since all man have the same natural light [une mesme lumière naturelle], it seems that they all must have the same notions [mesmes notions]." [90] This *lumen naturae* is nothing but a late reflection of Aristotle's "active intellect" (or St. Augustine's "divine illumination"?), which reminds us that, at least in the Averrhoist tradition, the active intellect was taken to be common to all men. Our more modest approach, appealing to some native ideas determined by the common genetic stock of mankind, is equally powerful to meet the challenge of linguistic relativism and, by the same token, to solve the problem of "radical translation." [91] We can understand our compatriots because we speak the same language, and we can learn the language of foreigners because we all carry a common heredity. Consequently we all share in the same human spirit. It is not an accident that the limits of mutual understanding coincide with the limits of human cross-fertility.

Mind

19. In no other matter is Descartes so seriously hampered by scholastic tradition and scholastic terminology and by his own

[89] *Principles*, I, 74; AT VIII, 37; HR I, 252.
[90] Oct. 1639: AT II, 598.
[91] See W. V. Quine, *Word and Object*, Chapter II.

religious beliefs as in his doctrine concerning the nature of the mind, the thinking thing. In spite of the latitude afforded him by such late scholastic novelties as "modes" and the various shades of "distinction of reason" (*distinctio rationis*), he is still fascinated by the overwhelming Aristotelian framework of essence and existence, substance and accident, matter and form —not to speak of the Christian dogma of personal immortality.

Yet he struggles manfully to express his insights; he twists or redefines scholastic terms, talks informally, often in metaphors, and indeed succeeds in shedding a good deal of the inherited burden. He no longer views the soul as the "form" of the body, pays only lip-service to the "faculties" of intellect and will, and, by using the respectable disguise of Suarez's modes, effectively identifies the sequence of thoughts with the mind itself. Finally, at least in the *Cogito* argument, even the distinction between essence and existence seems to lose its force. How disappointing is it then to see the soul re-enter the picture, not only as a shadowy "form" of the body but as a full-blooded substance, and assume its throne in the pineal gland, a scanner and an operator, a veritable ghost in the machine.

It is beyond my means in this book to psychoanalyze Descartes' schizophrenia in this matter. I can only guess that, in addition to his sincere religious beliefs, the reasons behind this unbelievable doctrine must have to do something with his confusion about sensation (i.e., the "influence" of the body on the soul) and his lack of attention to the nature of action (i.e., the "influence" of the soul on the body). My aim is more modest: I intend to show that his doctrine of the mind, and of the self, is perfectly understandable and plausible without the creation of any ghost, which is but a gratuitous (and inconsistent) addition to his theory. No wonder, then, that his followers, Spinoza, Malebranche, and Leibniz, were very quick to perform the necessary piece of exorcism.

Res Cogitans

20. "My essence consists solely in the fact that I am a thinking thing [quod sim res cogitans]." [92] "That substance in which thought immediately resides [cui inest immediate cogitatio] I call *Mind*." [93] "I understand that mind is something complete [rem completam] which doubts, knows, wishes, etc." [94] "The substance in which they [thinking activities] reside [cui insunt] we call a *thinking thing* or *the mind*." [95] These, and the many other definitions and descriptions of the mind that Descartes offers, can be understood in a perfectly orthodox manner: the soul is a complete substance, the *subiectum inhaesionis* of all its accidents, thus of all its acts, including the specific operations of thought, from which its definition is taken. This substance, however, remains really distinct (*distinctione reali*) from all these operations, which are nothing but actualizations of the soul's faculties (intellect and will), which themselves are really distinct from the substance. As the essence of the fiddler, as such, is defined in terms of fiddling, yet the acts of fiddling are distinct from the fiddler, so the essence of the thinker is defined in terms of thinking, yet the acts of thinking are distinct from the thinker.

Needless to say, this is not what Descartes means. The definition offered in the *Discourse*, and later inserted into the French version of *Meditation VI*, namely "a substance the whole essence or nature of which is to think [dont toute l'essence ou la nature n'est que de penser]," [96] and the definition in the *Principles*, "thought constitutes the nature [essence] of thinking substance," [97] let the Cartesian cat out of the scho-

[92] *Meditation VI*: AT VII, 78; HR I, 190.
[93] *Arguments* (after *Reply II*): AT VII, 160; HR II, 53.
[94] *Reply I*: AT VII, 121; HR II, 23.
[95] *Reply III*: AT VII, 176; HR II, 64.
[96] AT VI, 33; HR I, 101. AT IX, 62; HR I, 190.
[97] *Principles*, I, 53: AT VIII, 25; HR 240.

lastic bag: a mind is nothing but a temporally extended configuration of thoughts.[98]

"I do not see any other difference between the soul and its ideas, than between the piece of wax and the various shapes it can receive." [99] A schoolman might argue that the substance of the wax is really distinct from its shape, which is an accident. We hardly need to point out, however, that to Descartes this is but a distinction of reason: extension and material substance are one and the same thing in reality. If so, he is exposed to the following difficulty. When I heat a piece of wax, its extension (size and shape) changes. Yet, the scholastic would add —and Descartes too when he lets his mind run freely [100]—the wax remains the same. If, however, that piece of wax is nothing but a particular "mode" of extension, that is size and shape, then the wax cannot remain the same, for a changed shape is not the same shape and a changed size is not the same size. Consequently, if the mind were like a piece of wax, then any "change of mind" would amount to a change of identity.

Descartes meets the difficulty head on:

Body, regarded generally, is a substance, which is the reason why it also cannot perish, but the human body, inasmuch as it differs from other bodies, is composed only of a certain configuration of members and of other similar accidents, while the human mind is not similarly composed of any accidents, but is a pure substance. For although all the accidents of mind be changed, although, for instance, it think certain things, will others, perceive others, etc., despite all this it does not emerge from these changes another mind: the human body on the other hand becomes a very different thing

[98] Which is not so far from Hume's "heap or collection of different perceptions, united together by certain relations" (*Treatise* [Selby-Bigge edition], p. 207).

[99] Letter (to P. [Mesland]), May 1644: AT IV, 113.

[100] As in the wax passage of *Meditation II.*

from the sole fact that the figure or form of any of its portions is found to be changed.[101]

A particular extension, like my body or that piece of wax, does not remain the same through its changes. My mind, however, does. Consequently the mind is related to its particular acts not as a piece of wax is related to its successive shapes, but as the *"res extensa,"* the totality of the physical world, is related to its modes, that is, individual objects coexisting in space and succeeding one another in time. And, as the *res extensa* is the synthesis or totality of all objects rather than a distinct substratum that underlies them, so the *res cogitans* is the synthesis or totality of all of one's thoughts rather than a distinct substratum in which they inhere.

A letter to Arnauld makes this more explicit:

As extension, which constitutes the nature of body, greatly differs from the various shapes, or modes of extension, that it assumes [quos induit]; so thought, or thinking nature, in which, I think, the essence of human mind consists, is very different from this or that act of thought. . . . By thought, therefore, I do not understand a universal [concept], which would comprehend all modes of thought, but a particular nature [naturam particularem], which receives [recipit] all these modes, as extension too is a nature, which receives all shapes.[102]

The hands are still Esau's, but the voice is Jacob's: the phrases are scholastic, but the content is new. He still speaks as if extension were one kind of "stuff" that assumes various shapes, and thought another. He still cannot get away from the fascination of the "substratum" model to preserve unity through change. Yet, as the analogy of extension shows, he needs no substratum. The unity of the mind is like the unity of the world and not

[101] *Meditations*, Synopsis: AT VII, 14: HR I, 141.
[102] July 1648: AT V, 221.

like the unity of an Aristotelian substance: it incorporates, not merely survives, change.

21.   To us, free of the Aristotelian obsession, there are a number of analogies available to illustrate the kind of unity Descartes had in mind. Take a sine curve. As we move from the left to the right it changes (curvature, direction, etc.). Nevertheless it remains the same curve throughout, and not because of the existence of some underlying substratum. Or think of a chess game. It is not identical with any one of the individual moves; it embraces them all. And the fact that the game can change (an "open" phase, say, may follow a "closed" one) does not entail that some chess-stuff must sustain its identity. The spatial and temporal aspects may be combined, as they are in the case of a river, which changes from its source to its mouth in many ways, and from its birth to its death in many other ways, without—*teste* Quine and *pace* Heraclitus—any change of identity, and without the sameness of water or other stuff.

This last analogy is particularly suggestive: we indeed speak of the "stream" of consciousness. If the metaphor is apt, then the mind is the whole river, the totality of a systematically connected temporal stream of thoughts. None of these thoughts, and no subset of them, is identical with the mind; this does not mean, however, that they are but manifestations of an underlying substratum—a thought-stuff, soul-substance, or ghost. To have a mind is to have thoughts, and not to have something else that has them.

Not so with the body. Although it is true that I have my sensations (i.e., that sometimes I am in pain, feel hot, etc.), it is equally true that sometimes my stomach aches, my back hurts, my face feels hot, and my scalp itches. We never say, on the other hand, that something else thinks my thoughts (except metaphorically), that my head (or my intellect) understood something, or that my chest (or my will) decided to do something. In an exactly similar way, whereas I have the choice of saying either that I have formed or pronounced certain words, or that my mouth (lips, tongue, etc.) formed or pronounced certain words, I cannot say that my mouth said what I said, that it made a statement, gave an order, or the like; I must say that *I* made the statement, *I* gave the order, *I* said something. Thus, whereas I *have* something that has my sensations, and articulates my words—that is, I *have* a body—I do not have something that has my thoughts or issues them in speech-acts; *I* have them, and issue them immediately: I *am* a mind.

22. We are also accustomed to discontinuous wholes in space or time. What is the continuity of a chess game, when weeks may elapse between the moves (as in a correspondence game)? Or, where is the continuity in Eddington's table? To the medievals, however, nature abhors the void, and substances must be continuous in space and time. Descartes wholeheartedly subscribes to this view. As a result he must assume that the soul always thinks, since he cannot fall back on the reassuring "substratum" to bridge the thoughtless gaps in the mind's career. The mind's substance is thought, so think it must as long as it exists. "*You have a difficulty*, however, you say, *as to whether I think that the soul always thinks.* But why should it not always think, when it is a thinking substance?" he writes indignantly in *Reply* V. [103] And he insists that infants must think in their mothers' wombs since "nothing ever can be deprived of its own essence." [104] Nothing could show better the Cartesian identification of the soul with thought than this insistence on

[103] AT VII, 356; HR II, 210.
[104] Letter (to X), Aug. 1641: AT III, 423.

the necessity of continuous thought. For, I repeat, if he had merely regarded the soul as a thinking substance in the traditional sense, that is, as a substance whose specific operation is thinking, then he would not have found any difficulty in conceiving this "first actuality" subsisting through a stretch of time without any "second actuality," that is, actual thought.

Since to Descartes it is self-evident that "nothing can exist in the mind . . . of which it is not conscious," [105] he must conclude that a human being must be conscious, without interruption, throughout its entire life. This view lands him into all sorts of difficulties concerning consciousness in embryos and in people who are "unconscious," sound asleep, and so on. When faced with these troubles all he can offer is the lame explanation that people forget the thoughts they had while in these states.

I see no reason to agree with Descartes in this plainly absurd doctrine. As I just mentioned, the idea of discontinuous wholes is not at all repugnant. Moreover, we can even grant that a person, at least after he has reached the "age of reason," always has some thoughts, since such mental states as beliefs and intentions do not lapse even if the subject falls asleep or loses consciousness. What an unconscious person cannot do is to perform mental acts: he cannot notice, realize, or conclude that something is the case, and he cannot decide to do something or other. Notice that these acts, ideally at least, are instantaneous, so that even if we are actually thinking about a certain matter, the process is more similar to a succession of flashes than to a continuous glow.

Descartes, of course, never made the distinction, so central to our own discussion, between mental acts and mental states. Yet there are certain passages that indicate that he at least felt

[105] *Reply IV*: AT VII, 246; HR II, 115.

the need for such a distinction. Somewhat inconsistently, he seems to admit "unconscious" thoughts—that is, ideas that exist in the mind without its paying "attention" to them. Babies, he says, must have "the ideas of God, of themselves, and of all those truths that are called self evident [per se notae], no less than the adults, when they do not pay attention to them [ad ipsas non attendunt]." [106] "Our attention cannot remain continuously fixed on the same thing," [107] he writes to Elizabeth, yet, even if our attention turns away, that thought may remain in the mind:

> To be conscious is to think and to reflect upon one's thought; yet it is false that this cannot be done while a previous thought remains, since, as we saw, the soul is able to think many things simultaneously, to persevere in those thoughts, and, whenever it pleases, to reflect upon these thoughts, and thus to become conscious of them [queat . . . quotiescumque ipsi libuerit ad cogitationes suas reflectere, et sic suae cogitationis conscia esse].[108]

To escape inconsistency he once more falls back on the Aristotelian crutch, the distinction between act and potency.

> But it has to be noted that, while indeed we are always in actuality conscious of acts or operations of the mind, that is not the case with the faculties or powers [facultatum sine potentiarum] of mind, except potentially. So that when we dispose ourselves to the exercise of any faculty, if the faculty reside in us, we are immediately actually conscious of it [statim . . . fiamus eius actu conscii]; and hence we can deny that it exists in the mind, if we can form no consciousness of it [si eius conscii fieri nequeamus].[109]

The scholastic garb does not fit. Strictly speaking, the (intellectual) soul has two faculties, intellect and will, and these

[106] Letter (to X), Aug. 1641: AT III, 423.
[107] Letter (to Elizabeth), Sept. 1645: AT IV, 295.
[108] Replies (to Burman), Apr. 1648: AT V, 149.
[109] *Reply IV*: AT VII, 246; HR II, 115.

always reside in the soul. It is impossible, therefore, that Descartes should speak here of these faculties. What he speaks about are thoughts that are not "actual" in the way, say, realizations or decisions are actual, yet "exist in the mind potentially," inasmuch as we can become conscious of them, immediately, at will. What the scholastic garb hides, therefore, is nothing but the idea of mental states.[110]

A person, conscious or sound asleep, remains a mind, a configuration of thoughts, as long as he lives. From the fact that at certain times he is not "thinking about" anything (e.g., while asleep or watching television), it does not follow that there are times at which he has no thoughts at all, not even in the sense of "thinking that" something is the case, that something should be done, or the like. In a sense, then, it is true that the soul always thinks, notwithstanding the obvious fact that a person is not always conscious.

23. Immediacy, as we saw above, is Descartes' sole criterion of thought. The consideration of this point adds more weight to the hypothesis we have developed in the last two sections. If the mind, at any given time, is identical with a certain complex of thoughts—as a piece of wax at a given time is nothing but a configuration of certain modes of extension—then the very idea of a *medium* between the mind and its thoughts is impossible from the outset. Accordingly, it is an understatement to say that the mind *knows* its thoughts; the mind *is* these thoughts. And the usual question about the way of obtaining knowledge does not apply: the sentence *How do you*

[110] The scholastics themselves had some idea of mental states. Following Aristotle, they ascribed knowledge to the predicament of "quality" rather than "action," and regarded science as a "habit"—something like an intellectual "virtue"—rather than an activity.

know that you noticed (believe, want, etc.) such and such? has no use.

Descartes never ceases to insist that in all thoughts about anything whatever, the mind is "better known" than any other object. In thinking about the wax, he learns more about himself than about the wax, "since all the reasons which contribute to the knowledge of the wax, or any other body whatever, are yet better proofs of the nature of my mind!" [111] "Nothing yields the knowledge of so many attributes as our mind, because as many can be enumerated in its case as there are attributes in everything else, owing to the fact that it knows these; and hence its nature is best known of all [eius natura omnium est notissima]." [112] "It is impossible to think of anything without, at the same time, having an idea of our soul, as a thing capable of thinking whatever we think [comme une chose capable de penser tous ce que nous pensons] . . . since it is by it [par elle] that we conceive everything, it in itself is more conceivable than all the other things put together [elle seul plus concevable que toutes les autres choses ensemble]." [113] I do not claim that in these texts Descartes definitely implies the hypothesis outlined above. I do think, however, that these almost rhapsodic passages reveal an insight which, for obvious reasons, he was unwilling to voice, or even to admit to himself, in its undisguised form.

There are more specific passages that seem to derive from the same source. Consider this one, written just a few months before the text last quoted: "I believe that we have ideas not only of all of the things that are in our intellect, but even of everything that is in the will. For we could not want anything

[111] *Meditation II*: AT VII, 33; HR I, 157.
[112] *Reply* V: AT VII, 360; HR II, 213.
[113] Letter (to Mersenne), July 1641: AT III, 394.

without knowing that we want it, nor could we know it without an idea, *yet I do not suggest at all that this idea is different from the action itself.*" [114] He makes the same point in the *Passions:* "It is certain that we cannot desire anything without perceiving *by the same means* [par mesme moyen] that we desire it . . . yet . . . *this perception and this will are really one and the same thing.*" [115] These are about the most explicit texts I could find. What do they say? A mental act (be it of the understanding or of the will) is known without an idea that would be distinct from the act. The act itself is an idea, not an object of but a part of one's consciousness; it is, in an almost literal sense, a piece of one's mind. To be in the mind and to be known are the same thing: in this domain *esse est percipi*. And remember, being in the mind is not like being in a bottle, but like being in the world; not as something contained by a distinct receptacle, but as a real part of some totality.

The same approach explains the notorious passage in *Reply III:* "It is irrelevant to say, as this Philosopher [Hobbes] here does, that one thought cannot be the subject of another thought. Who, except my antagonist himself, ever imagined that it could?" [116] Earlier I remarked that, for example, the utterance *I say that I order you to go home* (if it is acceptable at all) amounts to the same speech-act as the utterance *I order you to go home*. Similarly, to think that *p* and to think that one

114 Letter (to Mersenne), Jan. 1641: AT III, 295 (my italics). Descartes here contradicts a passage from the *Discourse:* "For since the act of thought by which we believe a thing is different from that by which we know that we believe it, the one often exists without the other" (AT VI, 23; HR I, 95). He could not even escape the contradiction by claiming that this is a mere distinction of reason, for separability is the surest sign of a real distinction. He is obviously under a great strain in this point.
115 AT XI, 343; HR I, 340–341 (my italics).
116 AT VII, 175; HR II, 64.

thinks that *p* (if we can speak of such a thing) are the same thought.

Since ideas are thoughts, the same conclusions apply to innate ideas. They are not "in the mind" as in a distinct receptacle, they are the mind without the "adventitious" thoughts. "The mind acquires all his knowledge by reflecting either upon itself concerning the intellectual things . . . or . . . on the brain . . . ," Descartes writes to Mersenne,[117] and the same idea is repeated in *Meditation VI:* "Mind in its intellectual activity in some manner turns on itself, and considers some of the ideas which it possesses in itself." [118] There is but one step from here to Leibniz's famous *dicta: "Nihil est in intellectu, quod non fuerit in sensu,* excipe: *nisi ipse intellectus,"* [119] and "Nous somme innés, pour ainsi dire, à nous-même." [120] In our own terms: the inception of the human mind consists in the progressive emergence of the system of native ideas. This is true of the individual and, if we are allowed to speculate, must be true of the human race itself.

24. Despite the "special relation" Descartes admits between the soul and the body, he regards the soul as a complete substance, capable of existing and functioning without any aid from the body, which the soul merely uses as a workman uses his instrument.[121] Having thus abandoned the Aristotelian idea of the soul as the form of the body, he could not rely on the relation to the body to individuate the soul.

It seems to me that Descartes never even faced the problem

---

117 Letter (to Mersenne), Oct. 1639: AT II, 598.
118 AT VII, 73; HR I, 186.
119 *New Essays,* Book II, Chapter I, §2.
120 *Ibid.,* Book I, Chapter III, §3.
121 *Reply* V: AT VII, 354; HR II, 209.

of individuation with respect to the soul—that is, how to account for the numerical distinction between human minds. What makes my mind distinct from yours? The set of native ideas does not, since that, at least in its essentials, is common to all men. Is it then a matter of "adventitious" ideas? This Descartes could not allow, because these ideas enter the mind via the senses of the body, and the soul could exist and operate without them. He explicitly says this much in *Reply V*:

As you here ask me in such a straightforward manner, *what sort of idea I think my mind would have possessed either of God or of myself, if, from the time at which it was infused into the body, it had remained there with closed eyes and without employing any of the other senses,* I shall give you my answer ingenuously and candidly. I do not doubt that the mind under such circumstances . . . would have exactly the same idea of God and of itself as it now possesses, save only that these ideas would be much purer and clearer.[122]

If this is true of my mind, it must be true of your mind too; consequently you, too, would have a "pure and clear" idea of yourself in such a state. Unfortunately, however, we both would have the same idea—and the same mind.

In Chapter IV, I developed a solution which shows some affinity to the scholastic and the Leibnizian doctrine: minds are individuated by the subjective perspective that marks a significant portion of one's thoughts, which perspective is a function of the spatiotemporal continuity of one's sentient body. Consequently, in Descartes' terms, individuation is due to the existence of "adventitious" ideas.

This is, admittedly, a very un-Cartesian conclusion. Nevertheless there is a passage, at the very end of the *Meditations*, which is at least consonant with our findings. There Descartes tries to

[122] *Reply V*: AT VII, 375; HR II, 223.

dispel his own doubts, raised in *Meditation I,* about the possibility of discriminating dreams from reality.

If someone, while I was awake, quite suddenly appeared to me and disappeared as fast as do the images which I see in sleep, so that I could not know from whence the form came nor whither it went, it would not be without reason that I should deem it a spectre or a phantom formed by my brain rather than a real man. But when I perceive things as to which I know distinctly both *the place* from which they proceed, and that in which they are, and *the time* at which [unde, ubi et quando] they appeared to me; and when, *without any interruption, I can connect the perceptions which I have of them with the whole course of my life,* I am perfectly assured that these perceptions occur while I am waking and not during sleep.[123]

In this remarkably Kantian passage Descartes seems to establish a transcendental link between the full possession of the self, that is being awake, and the perception of "reality," that is the spatiotemporal unity of the manifold of experience. Unfortunately, as far as I know, this is his first and his last word on this topic. I wonder, incidentally, how Descartes could save the "reality" of afterlife in view of this passage. Will our disembodied experiences (say, in heaven or hell) fit into the spatiotemporal manifold, (let alone "without interruption")? If not, will they be like dreams? Whose dreams? Remember that the scholastic theologians had to invoke God's special intervention to vouchsafe the joys of heaven, and the agonies of hell, to the separated souls, which are in an "unnatural" state (*in statu violenti*) without their body.

Cogito

25. In recent years, particularly since Jaakka Hintikka's well-known paper,[124] a great deal has been written on the most

---

[123] AT VII, 89–90; HR I, 199 (my italics).

[124] "*Cogito, Ergo Sum:* Inference or Performance?", *The Philosophical Review,* LXXI (1962), 3–32.

famous of all Cartesian moves, the *Cogito* argument. I wish to end this chapter, and the book, by discussing this topic in the light of my own understanding of Descartes' psychology.

The two principal occurrences of the argument show a considerable difference in formulation. In the *Discourse* it runs as follows: "I noticed that whilst I thus wished to think all things false, it was absolutely essential that the 'I' who thought this should be somewhat, and remarking that this truth '*I think, therefore I am* [je pense, donc je suis]' was so certain and so assured that . . ." et cetera.[125] And in *Meditation II:* "We must come to the definite conclusion that this proposition: I am, I exist [ego sum, ego existo], is necessarily true each time that I pronounce it, or that I mentally conceive it." [126]

Descartes obviously regarded these two versions (and the many others scattered throughout his written work) as but different forms of the same argument. They occur at the same place in the corresponding structures of the *Discourse* and of the *Meditations,* and play the same role in the reasoning. Moreover, Descartes feels free to use variants of the first form in the very same *Meditation II.* "Of surety I myself did exist since I *persuaded* myself of something," [127] he writes just before giving the second form, and he argues, concerning the wax: "It certainly follows . . . that I exist myself from the fact that I *see* it; . . . it cannot be that when I see, or when I *think I see* [cogitem me videre], that myself who *think* am nought; . . . if I *judge* that the wax exists . . . the same thing will follow, to wit, that I am; and if I judge that my imagination . . . persuades me that the wax exists, I shall still conclude the same." [128] Furthermore, in *Reply II* he accepts the formulation "I think, hence I am, or exist";[129] in *Reply V* he writes, "From

[125] AT V, 32; HR I, 101.   [126] AT VII, 25; HR I, 150.
[127] *Ibid.* (my italics).   [128] AT VII, 33; HR I, 156 (my italics).
[129] AT VII, 140; HR II, 38.

the fact that I think [putem] that I walk I can very well infer the existence of the mind which so thinks [putat]";[130] and as late as in 1648 he still uses the form "Cogito ergo sum" in his replies to Burman.[131] Note, finally, that all his critics, from Gassendi to Burman, treat the argument in *Meditation II* as the same old *Cogito* argument.

26. I think it can indeed be demonstrated that all these forms amount to the same argument, or, to put it more exactly, are instances of the same argument-pattern.

The first thing we must realize is that the word *think* (penser, cogitare) functions in the argument as a generic verb, which can be cashed in for a variety of more specific verbs, such as *judge* (iudicare), *believe* (putare), *persuade oneself* (se persuadere), *wonder or doubt* (dubitare), and *see* (videre). This fact, of course, is in perfect harmony with Descartes' concept of thought, outlined in section 2 of this chapter. He himself puts it this way with respect to one specific verb, namely *doubt:* "For if it is true that I doubt just because I cannot doubt that I do so, it is also equally true that I think; *for what is doubting but thinking in a certain way?* And in fact if I did not think, I could not know whether I doubt or exist. Yet I am and I know that I am, and I know it because I doubt, *that is to say* because I think." [132] And later on, "*I doubt therefore I am;* or what comes to the same, *I think therefore I am.*" [133]

It immediately follows that the verb *cogitare* (or *penser*), in the *Cogito* argument, is not to be taken in the intransitive, but in the transitive sense, as a propositional verb. Therefore the phrase *cogito* (or *je pense*) is to be translated as *I think* (some-

---

130 AT VII, 352; HR II, 207.   131 AT V, 147.
132 *The Search after Truth:* AT X, 521; HR I, 322 (my italics).
133 *Ibid.:* AT X, 523; HR I, 324.

thing or other), and not as *I am thinking*.[134] Do not object that the verb *cogitare*, unlike its kin *putare*, is not a propositional verb in Latin. It is in Descartes' Latin. We just quoted "cogitem me videre" from *Meditation II*. Some other examples: "Iam ego concipio et cogito simul me loqui et me edere" [135] and "Quod autem istae ideae sint actuales . . . nec unquam scripsisse nec cogitasse." [136] *Penser*, of course, is also ambivalent in this respect.

Consequently the "*Cogito* argument" is nothing but the following argument-pattern:

I [think] . . . *p* . . . , therefore I am

which embraces a virtual infinity of individual arguments, such as

I wonder (whether *p*), therefore I am
I believe (that *p*), therefore I am
I judge (*a* to be *b*), therefore I am
I want (to *x*), therefore I am.

And, if the main thesis of this book is correct, then the *Cogito* argument will have a twin, namely the "*Dico* argument":

I [say] . . . *p* . . . , therefore I am

which comprises such members as

I state (that *p*), therefore I am
I order (you to *x*), therefore I am
I promise (to *x*), therefore I am.

In brief, *my existence follows from the thought or issuance of any proposition whatsoever.*

If I think, or state, that the cat is on the mat, and con-

---

[134] As it is in the Anscombe-Geach translation.
[135] Replies (to Burman), April 1648: AT V, 148.
[136] *Notes against a Programme*: AT VIII, 366.

Res Cogitans

clude that therefore I exist, I argue very well; if I decide to go to the theater, or promise to go with you, and hence conclude that I am, I reason correctly.

For example you have no right to make the inference: *I walk hence I exist*, except in so far as our awareness of walking is a thought; it is of this alone that the inference [illatio] holds good, not of the motion of the body, which sometimes does not exist, as in dreams, when nevertheless I appear to walk. Hence from the fact that I think that I walk [ex hoc quod putem me ambulare] I can very well infer the existence of the mind which so thinks [hoc putat], but not of the body which walks. So it is in all other cases.[137]

If one wants to conclude to one's existence from the sentiment or the opinion one has that one breathes, . . . even if this opinion is not true . . . one concludes very well; because this thought of breathing appears to our mind before the thought of our existence, and because we cannot doubt that we have it, when we have it. . . . And in this sense to say, *I breathe, therefore I am* is no other thing than to say *I think, therefore I am*.[138]

Thus the inference holds, even if the proposition conceived, or pronounced, is false, or has no truth-value. For my existence is not entailed by the content of that proposition but by my holding it or issuing it.

27. Consider, once more, the most general form of the *Cogito* argument:

I [think/say] . . . *p* . . . , therefore I exist,

where *p* stands for any proposition. Then substitute the conclusion, *I exist*, for *p* in the premise. We get

I [think/say] I exist, therefore I exist.

---

137 *Reply* V: AT VII, 352; HR II, 207.
138 Letter (to ***), March 1638: AT II, 37.

In other words: "This proposition: I am, I exist, is necessarily true each time that I pronounce it, or that I mentally conceive it." The argument given in *Meditation II* is an instance of the argument in the *Discourse*. Q.E.D.

28. To hit upon this fascinating application is an achievement worthy of Descartes' genius. To be able to follow him in this move, however, is an encouraging sign of the correctness of our interpretation of his psychology. And, I think, the same interpretation helps us to understand not only the form, but also the content of the *Cogito*.

Hitherto, in discussing this argument, we did not inquire into the connection between thinking and existence. Yet therein lies the whole sense of the argument. Descartes takes the easy way out in this matter. He claims that in the *Cogito* a person "does not deduce existence from thought by a syllogism, but, by a simple act of mental vision [simplici mentis intuitu], recognizes it as if it were a thing that is known *per se* [tanquam rem per se notam]." [139] There is nothing new, or surprising in this: the scholastics, too, regarded the maxim *agere sequitur esse* (action follows being) as self-evident. What he adds concerns the origin of the notions of thought and existence:

It is indeed true that *no one can be sure that he knows or that he exists, unless he knows what thought is and what existence is.* Not that this requires a cognition formed by reflection or one acquired by demonstration . . . It is altogether enough for one to know it by means of that internal cognition . . . which, when the object is thought and existence, is innate in all men.[140]

But what, we may ask, does the notion of existence add to the notion of thought? In other words, what is the point of

[139] *Reply II*: AT VII, 140; HR II, 38.
[140] *Reply VI*: AT VII, 422; HR V, 241.

the argument? "I think, therefore I think" is trivial; "I think, therefore I exist" is allegedly not. What is the difference?

There is this difference to begin with. *I think* in the argument is transitive, oriented toward the propositional content which I think. *I exist* is not: it is oriented, as it were, toward the subject that thinks. But what does it say about that subject? We ask this question, because we are accustomed to the idea that "existence is not a predicate" and thus has no content; whereas the sentence "Some cats do not purr" means something, the sentence "Some cats do not exist" does not. Consequently, in questions about existence, the issue is not whether a certain subject does or does not have a certain property, but whether a certain property, or set of properties, does or does not have a subject. For this reason, it is axiomatic that the issue of *quid sit* (what it is) must precede the issue of *an sit* (whether it is).[141] Yet it seems that Descartes first establishes that he is, and only then what he is (namely, a thinking thing). So that in the "conclusion" *I exist*, not only *exist* is empty, but *I* appears to be empty too. . . .

At this point we must recall what we discovered about the Cartesian doctrine of the mind, namely that the mind is not a distinct container of thoughts, but a temporally ordered structure of thoughts. To say, therefore, that one has a thought is to say that that thought is a part of a certain totality of thoughts. When I say, in giving (a particular version of) the *Cogito* argument, "I think (that *p*)," I say that the thought that *p* occupies the "present-slot" in a temporally ordered system of thoughts (which I indirectly denote by the word *I*); but when I conclude "therefore I exist," I say that there is a temporally

141 "According to the laws of true Logic, the question '*does a thing exist?*' must never be asked unless we already understand *what the thing is*," says Descartes himself (*Reply I:* AT VII, 108; HR II, 13).

ordered system of thoughts, the present-slot of which is occupied by that thought (obliquely referred to by the word *therefore*). These two assertions are, of course, logically equivalent. Not psychologically, however. As Descartes puts it in the "breathing" example recently quoted: "This thought of breathing appears to our mind before the thought of our existence." In thinking that *p*, I take myself for granted and am concerned with the proposition that *p*; in concluding that therefore I exist, I take that thought for granted and am concerned with the thinking subject. The beauty of the *Meditation II* version is that it unites these two steps: in thinking that I exist, I mentally assert the existence of a temporally ordered system of thoughts, the present slot of which is occupied by this very assertion.

Moreover—and I go beyond Descartes here—we know that the "fitting" of that thought into the framework of an individual consciousness is not just a matter of temporal succession. It must fit, insofar as it can, into a system of subjective perspective. This aspect alone makes it *my* thought. For, as Kant has shown, even the succession of time is but an aspect of the unity of one's thoughts. Accordingly, a thought belongs to me not because it merely follows a given sequence of thoughts, but because it conforms to a perspective determined by those thoughts.

Consider the following analogy. A point on a circle does not belong to the circle merely because it is contiguous to its neighboring points, but because it conforms to the same rule to which all the others conform, that of being equidistant from the center, or, equivalently, continuing the same curvature. Yet, given any segment of the circle, the function defining the whole is also given. The important thing is, however, that the function which defines that circle is neither a point nor a sequence of points; it is a thing of a totally different order, one and the same for all the segments. Similar relations hold, of course, between any curve and the function that defines it.

An individual mind, I would like to suggest, is like a curve; it contains many elements, many thoughts, but one and the same defining principle, namely a continuity of perspective, which, itself, is not a thought but a thing of a different order. Accordingly, the *I* may be taken, first, as nothing but the sum total of all of one's thoughts. In this sense I am identical with my mind: I *am* a mind. Second, it may be taken to denote the ordering or "generating" principle of the unity of a consciousness, which distinguishes it from all others and is itself not a thought or a sequence of thoughts but their "transcendental" subject. In this sense I *have* a mind. These two *I*'s correspond, of course, to Kant's phenomenal self and transcendental self. Finally, if we recall that the "function" that gives the individuality of a particular mind itself depends upon the spatiotemporal continuity of a sentient body (not to mention the body's role in action and speech), then we see the reason for yet another sense of the *I*, the one denoting the body. In this sense I *am* a body.

Returning to the *Cogito*, it seems to me that both *I*'s, in *I think* and in *I exist* refer to the transcendental *I*, the *I* that remains the same throughout my mental history. In saying (or thinking), "I exist," however, I ascribe to the same subject my phenomenal self—that is, all the thoughts in which my existence, as a mind, consists. "*Vita viventibus est esse* [life is the being of living things]" quoted the medievals Aristotle.[142] "*Cogitatio cogitantibus est esse* [thinking is the being of thinking things]" added Descartes.

The *Cogito* is, briefly, a dramatic account of the rise of self-

142 II *De Anima*, 415b.

consciousness. From the consciousness of my thought I become aware of myself, become "aware that I am, I think, I am a thinking thing." [143]

[143] *The Search after Truth:* AT X, 526; HR I, 327.

Appendix I

Shadow Performatives

There is a rather quaint little group of verbs that look like performatives ("expositives" to be more precise), yet do not have performative occurrences at all. I think of *allege, insinuate, hint, brag,* and, perhaps, *boast.* They are similar to performatives inasmuch as they are normally used to classify speech-acts. As I can say that Joe has stated, promised, or ordered something, or that he apologized about something or other, so I can say that he (or I, for that matter) has alleged or insinuated something, or bragged about this or that. What I cannot say, however, nor could anybody else, are things like

I insinuate that she was in his bedroom
I allege that I never saw her before
I brag that I am the best in the class.

The reason is obvious: the implications of these verbs (implying doubt, deviousness, or lack of due modesty) are such that by using them in the performative way the speaker would un-

dercut his own word. If, for instance, I were to say *I insinuate*
. . . , then I could not possibly be insinuating, for by saying
this I would reveal my intentions, which is incompatible with
the nature of an insinuation. Similarly, if I were to say *I allege*
. . . , I could not be alleging, for by thus casting doubt upon
what I was going to say, I could not claim credence for it,
which is essential to alleging. For these verbs the performative
use would be self-destroying, amounting to an "illocutionary
suicide." The situation is not quite so bad for *brag*, and still
less for *boast*.

The performative failure of *allege* is worth a still closer look.
The breakdown occurs because *allege*, like *state* and *assert*, and
unlike, say, *order* or *recommend*, puts the speech-act in the
dimension of truth—that is, claims belief rather than, say, obe-
dience or compliance. Yet, at the same time, it casts doubt
upon the truth of the allegation. These opposite forces operate
harmlessly in the nonperformative use: in saying that Joe alleged
something I say that he claimed belief for something which was
dubious. In the performative use, however, these forces would
clash: I would claim belief for something, adding that it is
unworthy of belief.

If this is so with *allege*, it must be worse—if that is possible—
with another very interesting verb, *lie*. Whereas the word *allegation* merely casts doubt upon what it is used to describe,
the word *lie* does more: it implies outright falsity. Consequently, as I cannot say *I allege* . . . and be alleging, *a fortiori*
I cannot say *I lie* . . . and be lying. For, to repeat, by saying
I lie . . . I would cancel the claim for belief, which, again, is
essential to lying. Moreover, obviously, the same illocutionary
suicide would result from the use of any device that tended
to undercut one's own credibility in a belief-claiming speech-

Appendix I

act. Thus even if one tries to assert *What I am saying now is false*, he will not succeed in asserting anything.

Finally, for the same reason, when the Cretan said that all Cretans were liars (i.e., that all statements made by them were false), he could not have meant to include that very statement, under penalty of breaking its assertive (i.e., belief-claiming) force—under penalty, that is, of spoiling it as a statement. It is possible, therefore, that what he said was true (if Cretans were indeed such a mendacious lot). Any subsequent statement to the effect that all Cretans are liars, however, would then be false, since our Cretan has made a true statement.

If you ask, "But what about *the* statement that all Cretans are liars?" I reply that there is no such thing *in abstracto*. Statements always belong to a person: they are somebody's statements. Consequently we do not have to worry about written "statements" accusing one another of falsity from opposite boxes on a piece of paper. They are not statements; they have no illocutionary force; no person stands behind them. There is no real "I" in front of the explicit performative their normal form would require.

Within a formal system, of course, the paradox may arise, and may have to be eliminated by equally formal means such as the introduction of metalanguages. The natural language, however, is free of this trouble.

Appendix II

Causative Constructions

Most intransitive verbs can appear in a transitive frame; for example:

John grows flowers
Mary bakes the cake
Joe walks the dog

and so on. These verbs are intransitive, since *Flowers grow*, *The cake bakes*, and *The dog walks* are complete sentences. With genuine transitives such an inversion fails. For example,

John pushes the cart

and

Mary holds the candle

do not have *The cart pushes* and *The candle holds* as counterparts. Yet, in some cases, even genuine transitives can be forced into the mold, provided an adverb is added: *The*

Appendix II

car drives easily, The horse rides smoothly. Some intransitives change slightly in the transitive frame: John fells the tree versus The tree falls, or Christ raises Lazarus versus Lazarus rises.

In accordance with intuition, I shall take it that it is the flower that really grows and not the gardener, and that it is the cake that really bakes and not the cook. These people only derivatively grow and bake. Accordingly, it is not The cake bakes that is, for example, a derivative of Somebody bakes the cake but the other way around. This second is to be derived along the lines of The cake bakes and somebody does it. This last sentence is a barbarism, but the idea is right. In more decent form, I suggest the following transformation:

$$(a_1) \quad N_i \, C \, (N_j \, V) - N_i \, V \, N_j.$$

C here stands for an abstract "causative" factor, semantically best approximated by make or cause. Making this more explicit, we obtain the variants:

$$(a_2) \quad N_i \, C \, (N_j \, V) - N_i \text{ makes } N_j \, V$$
$$(a_3) \quad N_i \, C \, (N_j \, V) - N_i \text{ causes } N_j \text{ to } V.$$

This way of looking at things has several advantages. First of all, it eliminates the need to talk about the so-called "middle voice": $N_i \, V \, N_j$ is a transformational product but $N_j \, V$, if it occurs at all (i.e., if V is intransitive), is not. Thus we maintain a sharp distinction between transitives and intransitives.

In addition, and more importantly, (a_1) leads us to the recognition of a very general pattern which operates beyond the limits of NV-kernels. Take the sentences:

John sharpened the knife
Mary blackened the window
Joe fattened the calf.

Quite obviously, something similar to (a_1) is true of these cases, namely:

(b_1) N_i C $(N_j$ *becomes* A$)$—N_i V_A N_j.

As above, there is another way of saying the same thing; for example:

> John made the knife sharp.

One can often be more specific by naming the action that gives A-ness to N_j. Thus we get things like

> John painted the wall green
> Mary fried the potato crisp
> Joe shot the girl dead.

This move has the advantage of supplementing (b_1) in case the A in question has no verb-derivative; we do not have *greenen*, *crispen*, or *deaden*, at least not in the desired sense. Thus it is useful to add

(b_2) N_i V_e $(N_j$ *becomes* A$)$—N_i V_e N_j A.

Needless to say that V_e and A have to be semantically matched, under penalty of deriving things like

> *John painted the window crisp
> *Joe shot the girl green

or other material for sick jokes.

Emboldened by our success, we ask next: what about N *is* N (or rather N *becomes* N) kernels? Indeed, we have at least one straight analogy to (b_1):

> The Queen knighted the captain

which exemplifies

Appendix II

(c$_1$) N$_i$ C (N$_j$ *becomes* N$_k$)—N$_i$ V$_{Nk}$ N$_j$.

There are many analogues to (b$_2$):

We elected him president

They named him commander

and so on. Thus (C$_2$) exists too:

(c$_2$) N$_i$ V$_c$ (N$_j$ *becomes* N$_k$)—N$_i$ V$_c$ N$_j$ N$_k$.

In this connection, the group of verbs containing *offer, give, donate, will,* and *leave* (property) deserves special consideration. The sentences

I gave him an apple

He left her the house

seem to conform to the product of (c$_2$). Yet, obviously, *become* would not work here: *come to have* (or simply *get*) is the correct substitute:

(c$_3$) N$_i$ V$_c$ (N$_j$ *comes to have* N$_k$)—N$_i$ V$_c$ N$_j$ N$_k$.

Since N$_j$ *has* N$_k$ has the synonym N$_k$ *belongs to* N$_j$, we will have a variant of (c$_3$):

(c$_4$) N$_i$ V$_c$ (N$_k$ *comes to belong to* N$_j$)—N$_i$ V$_c$ N$_k$ *to* N$_j$

which gives us the derivation of

I gave an apple to him

He left the house to her.

It is clear that the group of performatives that in Chapter II I called "operatives" conform to the pattern outlined in this appendix. Indeed, some troublesome operatives such as *knight* and *give* have already been mentioned and taken care of. The reason for this happy coincidence is not far to seek. The constructions covered in this appendix have one thing in common: they describe a "causative" situation—something happens under the influence of an agent that makes it happen. The cake bakes because the cook does something with it, the wall gets green because the painter does something to it, and the captain becomes a knight because the Queen *says* something to him. Furthermore, in most of these cases, what happens has a lasting effect: after the event the cake is baked, the wall is green, and the captain is a knight, regardless of what the cook, the painter, or the Queen does next. This is not necessarily so in the first category (a_{1-3}) above. The pilot flies the plane and the maid walks the dog. During these actions the plane is (being) flown (by the pilot), and the dog is (being) walked (by the maid). After the flight and the walk are over, however, the plane is not flown and the dog is not walked any more: they only have been flown or walked by somebody.

To put it quite clearly: the cake that once has been baked remains baked (it is now a baked cake), and the bottle that once has been broken remains broken (it is now a broken bottle); but the cart that once has been pushed does not remain pushed, and the bell that once has been rung does not remain rung. Notice that the sentence *The cart is pushed* and *The bell is rung* are but less idiomatic forms of *The cart is being pushed* and *The bell is being rung*. *The cake is baked* and *The bottle is broken*, on the other hand, do not mean *The cake is being baked* and *The bottle is being broken* at all. Moreover, whereas *The cart is (being) pushed* and *The bell is (being) rung* are genuine short passives, inasmuch as they admit the *by N* completion (*by the porter* or *by the butler*), *The cake is baked* and *The bottle is broken* do not admit such similar complements as *The cake is baked by the cook* and *The bottle is broken by the children*.

There is one more difference: by the baking the cake *be-*

Appendix II

comes baked and by the breaking the bottle *becomes* broken, much as by the painting the wall *becomes* green and by the knighting the hero *becomes* a knight. The cart, however, does not become pushed by the pushing and the bell does not become rung by the ringing; they do not, in fact, "become" anything at all by these things having been done to them: there is no lasting effect.

If *The cake is baked* and *The bottle is broken* are not short passives, what are they? The answer is clear: they are simple *N is A* sentences, which, accordingly, turn easily into AN-phrases: *baked cake, broken bottle.* This reminds us of (b₁); that is:

$$N_i \, C \, (N_j \, becomes \, A) - N_i \, V_A \, N_j.$$

Think of *widening the street* or *blackening the window.* Now I suggest its converse, namely,

$$(\beta) \; N_i \, C \, (N_j \, becomes \, A_V) - N_i \, V \, N_j$$

to account for all "permanent effect" verbs. *To break something* would be then, roughly, *to cause something to be broken.*

It may be objected that this move puts the cart before the horse: it derives the verb from the participle. But the force of this objection depends upon a too sharp, and too dogmatic, discrimination of word-classes. The morpheme *break*, I suggest, is per se neither a verb nor an adjective, but can appear in either role, donning as it does so the appropriate grammatical paraphernalia—much as the underlying semantic unit shared by, say, *fall* and *fell*, *bite* and *bait*, or *rise* and *raise* must transcend the transitive-intransitive distinction. Again, at least in the contemporary idiom, the "participle" *born* is rather more primary than the verb *bear* (in the relevant sense). Thus (β) should perhaps really be rewritten as

$$N_i \, C \, (N_j \, becomes \, A_W) - N_i \, V_W \, N_j$$

Appendix II

(where W stands for a neutral word-root). This, incidentally, will account for (b_1) too, and, in fact, it is also similar to (a_1). These analogies are worth elaborating: in (a_1) the verb V appears now in a transitive, then in an intransitive role; in (b_1) and in (c_1), when rewritten as suggested, the same root appears now in an adjective then in a verb. The same principle, of course—the "ambivalence" of certain roots—operates widely in the grammar of nominalizations and in other domains as well.

If this view is correct, then the seemingly trivial analysis I gave for some of the operatives in Chapter II, section 10, turns out to be by no means trivial. Take such verbs as *arrest* or *baptize*. Applying (β), we get

N_i C (N_j *becomes arrested*)—N_i *arrests* N_j
N_i C (N_j *becomes baptized*)—N_i *baptizes* N_j.

Consequently, to arrest somebody is to say (in the appropriate circumstances) *I arrest you* or, equivalently, (*I say*) *you are arrested* or (*I say*) *you are under arrest*. Similarly, when the boss says to the employee, in firing him, *You are* (*hereby*) *fired* rather than *I* (*hereby*) *fire you*, he knows what he is doing.

Appendix III

The Last Word of Empiricism

The account I gave of innate (or rather "native") ideas is open to an obvious objection. One could argue that although this theory might explain the ease children display in learning a language and thus may have some importance for scientific psychology, with respect to the philosophical problem of ideas it offers no solution—it merely pushes the problem further back in time. By suggesting that these ideas are native *in individual humans* (as we know them now), one does not say anything about the absolute origin of these ideas, that is about their genesis *in the human race*. In consequence, we are still up in the air concerning their relation to the world, that is their possible dependence upon the physical environment and their representative value.

This is in contrast with the traditional theories of innate ideas. Plato, for instance, does establish a connection between our ideas and the world, by claiming that both of these domains are derived from a common source, the realm of eternal ideas, via recollection in our case, and via the "imitative" work of the creator Demiurge with respect to the visible world. Descartes, on the other hand, invokes God's veracity to the same end: God, the creator of the world and of our souls, would be a deceiver if he had equipped the latter with sets of "wrong" ideas.

Where Descartes, and his age, appealed to God, we appeal to evolution. To them, it was God who provided his creatures with the necessary equipment—teeth and claws, instincts and ideas—for their appropriate form of life; to us, mutations and natural selection can do the same. For if ideas are neurologically based, as I believe they are, then there is no reason to suppose that the process of evolution somehow failed to operate on this most important base for human life. If claws and teeth, senses and native reflexes, have survival value, how much more value must a native conceptual framework enabling man to deal with the world, with himself, and with his fellows have. It is bad enough that we are born as a "naked ape" in the body; why should we start out with a *tabula rasa* for a mind as well?

I suggest, therefore—but, of course, cannot prove—that the system of native ideas has evolved in the same way as any other part of the native human endowment. And, like any other part, it is subject to improvement and extension as a result of transmitted culture and individual effort. As microscopes are related to natural sight, as tools to manual skill, so is related (for example) non-Eucledian geometry to our native ideas of extension.

If this is true, then empiricism has the final word. For evolution is governed by the environment: man's native equipment, including his ideas, has developed in response to the demands of the physical world. Does this entail that ideas must be "similar" to things in the world? No more than a saw is similar to the log it cuts, or a sales-curve to the activities it represents. The last word of empiricism is a feeble one.

Works Cited

Aquinas, St. Thomas. *In Boethium de Trinitate*, Questions V–VI, translated in Armand Maurer, ed., *The Division and Methods of the Sciences*. Toronto: The Pontifical Institute of Mediaeval Studies, 1958.

Augustinus, St. Aurelius. *De Magistro*, trans. George G. Leckie, in *Concerning the Teacher and On the Immortality of the Soul*. New York: Appleton-Century-Crofts, 1938.

Austin, J. L. *How to Do Things with Words*. Oxford: Clarendon Press, 1962.

Chomsky, Noam. *Cartesian Linguistics*. New York: Harper and Row, 1966.

——. *Language and Mind*. New York: Harcourt, Brace and World, 1968.

——. "Linguistics and Philosophy," in Sidney Hook, ed., *Language and Philosophy*. New York: New York University Press, 1969, pp. 51–94.

Descartes, René. *Oeuvres*, ed. Charles Adam and Paul Tannery. Paris: Cerf, 1897, 1913.

——. *The Philosophical Works of Descartes*, trans. and ed. Elizabeth S. Haldane and G. R. T. Ross. Cambridge: At the University Press, 1967.

219

Works Cited

——. *Philosophical Writings*, trans. and ed. Elizabeth Anscombe and Peter Thomas Geach. London: Nelson, 1954.

——. *Selections*, ed. Ralph M. Eaton. New York: Charles Scribner's Sons, 1927.

Fillmore, Charles J. "Types of Lexical Information," in Danny D. Steinberg and Leon A. Jakobovitz, eds., *Semantics*. Cambridge: University Press, 1971, pp. 370–392.

Grice, H. P. "Meaning," *Philosophical Review*, LXVI (1957), 377–388.

Hintikka, Jaakko. "*Cogito, Ergo Sum:* Inference or Performance?" in *Philosophical Review* LXXI (1962), 3–32.

Hume, David. *A Treatise of Human Nature*, ed. L. A. Selby-Bigge. Oxford: Clarendon Press, 1888.

Kant, Immanuel. *Critique of Pure Reason*, trans. Norman Kemp Smith. London: Macmillan, 1953.

Katz, Jerrold J. *The Philosophy of Language*. New York: Harper and Row, 1966.

Lakoff, George. "On Generative Semantics," in Danny D. Steinberg and Leon A. Jakobovitz, eds., *Semantics*. Cambridge: At the University Press, 1971, pp. 232–296.

Lees, Robert B. *The Grammar of English Nominalizations*. The Hague: Mouton, 1960.

Leibniz, Gottfried Wilhelm von. *Selections*, ed. Philip P. Wiener. New York: Charles Scribner's Sons, 1951.

Lennenberg, Eric, H., ed. *New Directions in the Study of Language*. Cambridge, Mass.: M.I.T. Press, 1964.

McCawley, James D. "Meaning and the Description of Languages," in Jay F. Rosenberg and Charles Travis, ed., *Readings in the Philosophy of Language*, pp. 514–533. Englewood Cliffs, N. J.: Prentice-Hall, 1971.

Postal, Paul. "On the Surface Verb *Remind*" in *Linguistic Inquiry*, I (1970), 37–120.

Quine, Willard Van Orman. *From a Logical Point of View*. New York: Harper and Row, 1963.

——. *Word and Object*. New York: Technology Press and John Wiley and Sons, 1960.

Ross, J. R. "On Declarative Sentences," in R. Jacobs and P. Rosen-

Works Cited

baum, eds., *Readings in Transformational Grammar*, pp. 222–272. Waltham, Mass.: Blaisdell, 1970.

Russell, Bertrand. *An Inquiry into Meaning and Truth.* New York: Norton, 1940.

Ryle, Gilbert. *The Concept of Mind.* New York: Barnes and Noble, 1949.

Smith, Frank, and George A. Miller, eds. *The Genesis of Language.* Cambridge, Mass.: M.I.T. Press, 1966.

Strawson, P. F. *Individuals.* London: Methuen, 1959.

Vendler, Zeno. *Adjectives and Nominalizations.* The Hague—Paris: Mouton, 1968.

———. "Causal Relations," *Journal of Philosophy* LXIV (1967), 704–713.

———. *Linguistics in Philosophy.* Ithaca, N.Y.: Cornell University Press, 1967.

Wittgenstein, Ludwig. *The Blue and Brown Books.* Oxford: Basil Blackwell, 1964.

———. *Philosophical Investigations.* New York: Macmillan, 1960.

———. *Tractatus Logico-Philosophicus.* London: Routledge and Kegan Paul, 1961.

Whorf, B. L. *Language, Thought and Reality: Selected Writings of Benjamin Lee Whorf,* ed. John B. Carroll. Cambridge, Mass.: M.I.T. Press, 1956.

Index

223

Index

Index

Library of Congress Cataloging in Publication Data
(For library cataloging purposes only)

Vendler, Zeno.
  Res cogitans.

  (Contemporary philosophy)
  Bibliography: p.
  1. Analysis (Philosophy) 2. Descartes, René,
1596–1650. 3. Thought and thinking. 4. Speech.
5. Meaning (Philosophy) I. Title. II. Series:
Contemporary philosophy series.
B808.5.V45   153.4   72–3182
ISBN 0–8014–0743–5